AFFLICTIONS & DEPARTURES

Other books by Madeline Sonik
Stone Sightings (poetry)
Arms (a novel)
Drying the Bones (stories)
Belinda and the Dustbunnys (children's novel)

{Essays}

Madeline Sonik

ANVIL PRESS * VANCOUVER * 2011

Anvil Press Publishers Inc.
P.O. Box 3008, Main Post Office
Vancouver, B.C. V6B 3X5 Canada
www.anvilpress.com

Disclaimer: While this is a work of nonfiction, many names have been changed to protect people's privacy.

Library and Archives Canada Cataloguing in Publication

Sonik, Madeline, 1960–
   Afflictions & departures : essays / Madeline Sonik.

ISBN 978-1-897535-67-7

   I. Title. II. Title: Afflictions and departures.

PS8587.O558A34 2011   C814'.6   C2011-901457-2

Cover design by Dave Barnes
Interior design by HeimatHouse

Represented in Canada by the Literary Press Group
Distributed by the University of Toronto Press

  Canada

The publisher gratefully acknowledges the financial assistance of the Canada Council for the Arts, the Canada Book Fund, and the Province of British Columbia through the B.C. Arts Council and the Book Publishing Tax Credit.

Printed and bound in Canada.

For Madison, my birth buddy and heart mate.

ACKNOWLEDGMENTS

I wish to thank, first and foremost, my partner Eric Henderson, who has been my stalwart first reader and editor over these many long years. I also wish to thank Andreas Schroeder at the University of British Columbia, who got me to write the first essay in this collection and explained to me how constructing a collection of essays is like constructing a house.

George McWhirter and Renee Norman were two teachers who kept the flame of the essays alive during my remaining UBC years, and Tony Barrett, also from UBC, asked me many inspiring questions and made excellent editing suggestions for several of these essays.

I wish also to thank Sharon Young, who responded to my many requests for interlibrary loan microfilm, as well as all the librarians at the Greater Victoria Public Library and the University of Victoria's McPherson Library, who assisted with my research.

Thanks also go out to all the editors of the literary magazines that published earlier forms of these essays: *Event, Prairie Fire, The Bellingham Review, Grain, Prism International, subTerrain, Windsor Review,* and *Descant.*

And last but not least, thanks to Brian Kaufman and Aimee Ouellette at Anvil for their suggestions and care.

CONTENTS

When stories are not told, we risk losing our way. Lies trip us up, lacunae gape like blanks in a footbridge. Time shatters and, though we strain to follow the pieces like pebbles through the forest, we are led farther and farther astray. Stories are replaced by evidence. Moments disconnected from eras. Exhibits plucked from experience. We forget the consolation of the common thread—the way events are stained with the dye of stories older than the facts themselves. We lose our memory. This can make a person ill. This can make a world ill.

—Ann-Marie MacDonald

FIRST PASSAGE

IMAGINE, THE QUEEN MARY, 81,237 gross tons of steel, wood, and homey comforts, coursing through the codfish-grey Atlantic. Although it is mid-August, the sun's sheathed in a misty halo. Cabin-class passengers in neat white sweaters and suit jackets brace sturdy deck chairs, accept warm plaid blankets and hot tea. The chill off the ocean is numbing, yet for most this is a once-in-a-lifetime trip.

The year is 1959. On the 21st of August, less than a week away, Hawaii will become the fiftieth state in the union. Few here know or care about this. The brackish air fills their nostrils, the icy mist puckers their flesh. The ship pitches and rolls like a thousand-foot cradle and the passengers murmur their contentment.

The first-class restaurant, located on deck R, is plush and elegant. There are twin brass doors, a parquet floor—and the food! The food alone is worth the price of the passage: grapefruit au kirsch, croquette of duckling, sauce mousseline for halibut, roast turkey, devilled ham, orange soufflé. There are 2,400 bottles of champagne aboard for this journey, and an equivalent amount of Scotch and aperitifs. Black ties and evening gowns are worn in the dining room; after dinner there is dancing.

Imagine my parents on the *Queen Mary*. My father's name is Boris, and my mother's name, the same as mine—Madeline. They are spinning and laughing together on the dance floor. My mother is wearing black, high-heeled shoes with ankle straps; her dress is one she made herself, gold and burgundy with long satin sleeves. My father smells of sweet aftershave. He smiles; he has a space between his two front teeth, like me. My parents are returning to the United States, instead of going to Switzerland where my father was offered a second chance. They are taking the *Queen Mary* "home," although "home" for my mother is really Manchester, England. For my father, it's Canada, unless he's been drinking—then it's Russia. They are dancing and giggling, gulping champagne, recalling together how they met, how my father first danced with my mother on a bet. It is a starry evening, yet warm. The winds from the north have died away, and a bubble of silence contains them. My parents stroll the promenade deck arm in arm. It is 724 feet long and feels to them deliciously endless. Memories, champagne, and this great expanse of ship allow them to avoid discussion of the future. There are twelve decks, a Turkish bath, a cinema, a shopping arcade, and a chapel. It is three a.m.; nothing on board is open. The dance band packs away their violins, their cello, their soft drums. My parents go to their cabin on deck M. It is 1959, the year the Dalai Lama flees Tibet.

They fling open their cabin door, teeter at the threshold, fall upon the soft double bed. Only the thrum of the engine, the crinkling of my mother's gown, the slap of my father's shoe falling hard to the floor can be heard. It is 1959, a year before birth control pills are made available to women, twenty-three years before the AIDS epidemic makes condoms accessible everywhere and politically correct. The sun is rising through a starboard hatch. My parents wake with splitting heads. My father hunts down a cabin steward for Aspirin and coffee. My mother stumbles to the bathroom and retches in the toilet, trying to remember the night before. The *Queen Mary* glides like a sharp knife dividing the surface blackness of water into separate fields, surrounding itself with white steaming spume.

Three months from now, my mother will be told by a doctor in Detroit she is pregnant.

Imagine me, a few splitting cells in my mother's belly, a fraction of a millimetre across, an alien life form making my way down her fallopian tube in order to leach blood from her cushioned nest. It will be six weeks before my sexual identity emerges, before the XX combination of my chromosomes unfolds, before my mother starts to question the lateness of her period, the tremendous inescapable nausea of her mornings that began on the ship and didn't end for eight months. It is 1959, three years before the structure of DNA is discovered, twenty-one years before recombinant DNA technology will make it possible to add moth genes to tomatoes in order to prevent them bruising. In the future, there will be controversy over the speed with which genetically manufactured crops are marketed. A modified corn crop in the United States will prove lethal to harmless monarch butterflies. Its toxin will show up in organic corn chips imported to Europe. No one will have considered that corn pollen naturally blows beyond the cornfield in which it occurs. But this is a problem for the future, one my mother will not be alive to witness.

Right now, my mother is combing her thinning hair, looking into the bathroom mirror, considering my father. He's broken his contract in England, quit his job, told his bosses he's tired of being told where to live. His company was good to him, though. Even after he refused to go to Switzerland, they paid his way home. My mother wonders, while damaged black strands of her permanent waved hair fall into the gleaming sink, if she made a mistake in marrying him. It is a fleeting thought, and she turns on the tap, washes her severed hair away, puts on red lipstick.

The ship leans and lunges over unknowable grey depths. Somewhere, beneath us, there are mountains. Small finned herring and mackerel swim. A few years before this voyage, stabilizers were installed on the ship to stop her from rolling on her side and hanging there. Imagine waiters carrying trays at thirty-degree angles, of third-class passengers falling down stairs; their stairwells, unlike those in cabin class, have no safety rails.

My mother drinks a glass of water, yet still feels queasy. Her hangover, her motion sickness, will last for the next eight months. The doctor she will visit in Detroit will offer her samples of thalidomide, which some intuitive part of her will reject, although my father, angrily, will call her "martyr," and they will argue for the rest of her pregnancy. I will be born on May 12th in an inner city hospital, which will metamorphose to a psychiatric institution, then a drug rehab centre, before finally being torn down to accommodate a freeway. My father will get a job with New York Central Railroad, we will move to Cleveland, Ohio, then Chicago, but my father will never again find a job that pays as much as the one he left in England. In spite of his dislike of travel, he will frequently be away on business. The night I am born, he will be in Milwaukee. My mother will curse him as I take my first breath. She will damn him, every time she remembers how she had to struggle into a taxi all alone, in the middle of the night, damp footed, with amniotic fluid staining her precious alligator shoes. Often, over the course of the next fourteen years, she will know regret. She will waste years starching and ironing bed sheets, my father's white cotton handkerchiefs and shirts, though "wash and wear" clothing has been available since the summer of 1952.

The Civil Rights Act will be passed in 1964 and will prohibit the discrimination against women by any company with twenty-five or more employees. My mother will not work outside the home until I am ten, when my father is fired from his accounting job at the railroad. She will make a mere one hundred dollars a week as a sales clerk and become the breadwinner of the family.

My father will spend a good part of the summer of 1970 at the dining room table typing his resumé with one finger, shouting for me to make him screwdrivers. I will spend the summer trying to figure out ways to avoid him, or at least keep him sober. I will serve him drinks made with only a quarter of a shot of vodka; I will pour half a bottle of vodka down the sink and replace it with water; I will drop the bottle on the floor and smash it.

My mother doesn't have a driver's licence and will never get one. At five o'clock she will finish work. My father will inevitably be too drunk to pick her up. She'll make her way home on the bus. When she arrives, I will be hiding under blankets in my bedroom closet. My father will be breaking things in the kitchen. For the rest of their married lives, my father will be a violent alcoholic. He will chase me all over the house and try to push my mother down the stairs. In some states, a woman who shoots and kills her husband is accused of "homicide," while a man who shoots his wife has committed a "passion shooting." My mother tells me often that she plans to leave my father, but she never does. My parents sell the house, because one hundred dollars a week barely buys groceries. They have gone into debt to make mortgage payments and buy vodka, and by the winter of 1970 my father will still be unemployed.

The *Queen Mary* slices water, drives through peaks and valleys of unremitting green. The rudder of this vessel weighs 140 tons. For every thirteen feet it travels, its engine uses one gallon of fuel. Imagine the cerulean sky suffocating in its openness, the dizziness of passengers who panic for dry land. Although there is daylight, it is like darkness, overwhelming. Twenty-four lifeboats, suspended near the funnel ailerons, moaning and creaking, protesting their emptiness.

It is 1959, and I am a bundle of symmetrical cells that looks something like a blackberry, tumbling down a slide, finding my way to ground. This earth, I find, is lush in its pinkness, sweet in its blood. Already, it is determined I will have my father's small pupils, his analytic gaze, his hair, his voice. My mother will bequeath her lips, her tiny nose, for which I will be ridiculed all my days of grade school, and with which I will later curse one of my own two daughters. It is 1959, and American Airlines starts its 707 service from New York to Los Angeles. Before the year is out, the USSR will have sent a translunar satellite to photograph the far side of the moon.

By day, my mother takes advantage of the shopping arcade and the ship's pool, while my father plays shuffleboard and drinks. Both my parents are thirty years old, and already have a sense of life's inevitability. Both fear death. In the next dozen years, my mother will put an additional 150 pounds on her small frame. My father will make reference to her weight when he's drinking, which will always make her cry.

Eight years after this voyage, the *Queen Mary* will be sold to the city of Long Beach, turned into a floating conference centre and hotel. Large parts of her will be gutted, transformed. Candy machines and litter will diminish the elegance of the first-class dining room, and third-class cabins will be used for storage.

In 1973, we will be living in Ontario, the place of my father's birth. He will be a discontented loans officer, and will lose his job once again before discovering he has cancer of the colon. After surgery, chemotherapy, and radiation, he will remain in hospital. My mother will not go to visit him. I will go instead, to watch over him in his coma, and notice how he dies. In the years that follow, I will drop out of school and work in England, come back to Canada, and start a family. My mother will die of a heart attack in 1986. And when I am cleaning her house, in preparation for its sale, I will find pictures and menus from this voyage on the *Queen Mary*, and a small leather-bound journal, which begins, "Imagine…the *Queen Mary!*" And I will.

KOREAN MOON

BEFORE I AM BORN, my father will wear a shirt that is patterned with red valentine hearts and arrows. He will stand in the living room of a house I will never know, holding my brother, his infant son. At night, when the baby wakes, my father, unable to sleep, will go to the basement and work on large paint-by-number canvases of East Asian scenes: fishermen in flat brown hats, red pagodas, azure mountains, willowy black-haired women in kimonos with parasols. It is 1956, and the smell of linseed oil clings to his hands. If he knows about the critical judgments hurled at this popular art form, they do not faze him. He is content, for now, to stay within the lines, to forgo any sense of choice or option, to free his mind in the minute motions of perfunctory brush strokes, and later, to build frames for his masterpieces and to hang them on his living room walls.

Earlier this decade, President Eisenhower's appointment secretary had the idea of creating a White House paint-by-number gallery. He handed out kits to visitors and officials alike. J. Edgar Hoover was just one of the gallery's contributors. He completed a canvas of a Swiss village, in which a brown-roofed church stands nestled between houses on a smooth, green hill slope before a range of mountains.

My father has never seen this picture, never heard about this "do-it-yourself" gallery, but even if he had, he would never think of saying: "What's good enough for the White House is good enough for me." The Korean War is over. He has been back in North America for a year and three months. He has nothing but contempt for politics and patriotism, and nothing but a bad conscience over his own involvement in the war. His motives for enlisting were entirely self-serving. He did not choose to become a soldier to protect "the land of the free" but rather to take advantage of the G.I. Bill of Rights that had come into being in 1944, offering tuition, books, and subsistence to veterans who wished to continue their education. He was not even born in the United States, but in Windsor, Ontario, to a Russian father and a Ukrainian mother, neither of whom had ever learned English but instead had created their own household language from disparate variants of the languages they knew. They planted fruit trees and a vegetable garden in the backyard of their house, and kept a cow for milk and chickens for eggs. As a boy, my father sold fruit and puppies door to door, and ran away from home once when, accidentally, he sold his mother's best plums at the price of the ordinary ones. He had been so ashamed that he hadn't been able to face her, and when he finally returned, he was even more ashamed because of the grief his disappearance had caused.

In later years, when my siblings and I are old enough to listen, he will tell us how his mother's hair and flesh turned chalk white in his week-long absence. How she cried and wrung her hands and made him promise on her grave that he would never do such a thing again. He will not tell us what he did or where he went during his self-imposed exile, just as he will never give us a serious account of his occupation as a soldier in the Korean War.

When I am growing up, the houses we live in will never exhibit evidence of my father's military years. There will be no plaques with eagles and no shadow boxes displaying medals as I see in the homes of my friends. These things reside in my grandmother's house in Canada, across the border, and are so foreign to me there that for many years I do not even associate them with my family. The ornate Japanese lamp on my grandmother's end table, the beautiful hand-painted jewellery box in her room, the etched brass vase that graces the window ledge of her sun porch, all of these peculiar things fascinate, but I have no idea of their origins or that they carry a piece of silent history that I will one day regret not knowing.

I have only glimpses of my father's past—memories and stories, like scattered bones which I attempt to gather from the clay of childhood and assemble into some comprehensive design. I want to find a larger way of seeing both his life and mine, and understanding the measure of experience and the resonance of its impact over time.

In the houses of my childhood, in all of the bedroom closets that my father has ever had, there hangs a velvet robe the colour of golden poppies. It is lined and lapelled with satin burgundy brocade, with dragons and phoenixes, and contrasts conspicuously with the blacks and greys of his business suits. One day, when I am playing hide and seek, I find it and ask him what it is and when he got it. I have never seen him wear it. "A smoking jacket from Korea," he tells me, and I go to smell it, to see if I can detect the fragrance of smoke. This is the first time I hear him use the word *Korea*, a word that to my preschool ears sounds as unpleasant as *diarrhea*, and I am disappointed that such a beautiful robe should have associations with such a distasteful word. "Where is Korea?" I ask him, and he takes me to his globe in the study to show me the small neck of land the colour of olives, protruding from China. "I was a stamp collector there," he tells me, and goes to the bookshelf where he picks up an album containing hundreds of colourful stamps. I see him in my mind's eye, a contemporary Johnny Appleseed, walking through valleys of tall green grass—but instead of disseminating orchards, he is gathering these precious patches of paper, rectangles of sticky fruit, abandoned by letters like dross.

My father confirms my suspicions that the country's name does indeed have a connection with "diarrhea" when he tells me about the portable toilets (honey-buckets) that soldiers used. Local farmers would purchase their "honey" to fertilize crops. Though the crops looked very healthy, they often contained bacteria and worms that would make people sick and sometimes even kill them. Later, he tells me about the extremes of hot and cold, of hungry refugee children, half-naked in the snow, who come begging soldiers for K rations. "There was one little boy who was crippled," he recounts, "and a soldier pushed him into a pile of trash. The other soldiers laughed," he continues, until my eyes fill with tears.

"But what did you do?" I demand from him, and he knows that he can only give the following answer: "I helped him up and gave him some K rations." True or false, his words allow me to stop crying.

My father does not tell me that US soldiers were ordered to slaughter South Korean refugees—that they machine-gunned old women and small children because they might have been Northern spies. If my father knows about such things, he does not speak of them. It is decades before anyone publicly will.

"Did you ever kill anyone when you were a soldier?" I ask, hoping he will tell me "No."

"I collected stamps," my father says.

And the image of a contemporary Johnny Appleseed reasserts itself, but this time wearing a combat helmet and army boots, stepping gingerly over portable toilets, disseminating K rations to crippled children in the same green valley where he gathers stamps.

I am too young to understand the complexities of war, to be told of a land controlled and oppressed by strangers, then carved up by decision makers who did not take into account the symbiosis of a nation. I am too young to comprehend sanctioned killing and destruction, too youthfully honest to entertain the idea that torturing and bullying others into submission is sometimes the only way a country can settle its disputes or satisfy its greed. Such concepts would never pass muster in playschool. But I am not too young to envision some of war's horrors, to understand that napalm is a jellied blend of chemicals and gasoline that can burn longer and hotter than fire. I am not too young to imagine how containers of napalm were dropped from planes onto buildings and people. For weeks, I have nightmares of jellied blobs of fire sticking to the clothes and flesh of faceless people, turning them to ash. I tell my father these dreams when I wake up in the middle of the night. Sometimes his restlessness wakes me, too, and I discover him in the wee hours of the morning in quiet contemplation, smoking cigarettes at the dining room table.

Hidden in the basements of the houses where we live, there is a box that contains mementos from his past: a pearl-white Korean/English dictionary; an abacus made from ivory and bamboo; a large black-paged photograph album and three bundles of letters tied with red ribbon. The box is private and my brothers and I know we aren't to touch it, but one day the temptation grows too strong. Before we are discovered, we see pictures of my father, dressed in khaki. He stands in front of barbed wire. The soil under his heavy black boots is barren and dusty. These pictures contrast markedly with others in the album in which he is in a wooden boat, paddling on a lake with a beautiful East Asian woman. There are some pictures just of her, surrounded by lush green trees and flowers. Her hair is long and black, her face serene. When my father discovers us, he takes the album from my hands and wordlessly packs it away. He then seals the box with moving tape and tells us firmly that his personal things are off limits.

There are secrets that my father holds. Secrets of his past that he will never reveal. In 1974, when he dies at age forty-five, he bequeaths a chasm in his history, a vacuity which my speculations will endlessly attempt to fill. Through the years, there will be stories—how my father got his brother to do his army aptitude test. How the test's results pigeonholed him into a life as an accountant, a life he was never suited for.

Over the years, there will be revelations: my father's private box of memories torn open, bundles of letters spilled from their ribbons, a woman's consistent greeting to my father as "Dearest husband."

"She was a Korean woman," my mother will tell me. "She was your father's girlfriend…when he was over there." The golden smoking jacket had been a gift from her, and my mother resented his keeping it. Now that he's dead, she sends it off to the Goodwill, collects the letters and photographs from his box, makes a fire in the backyard and burns them all.

"He always intended to go back to that woman," my aunt will tell me, years later. "Your grandparents begged him not to go. 'What kind of life could you have? What kind of children would you bring into the world? No one wants a mixed child," my aunt wrinkles her nose. I imagine my father's loneliness in his initial weeks back home, his sense of unreality and the overwhelming burden of the choices he has made—the choices he must make.

He meets my mother at a YMCA social. On a bet, he asks her to dance. His buddies, former soldiers, wager she won't dance with him—but she does, and for an evening he is able to forget Korea, forget the unpleasantness of war and the pressures of the incongruent worlds that he inhabits. The following day, they meet again, and then again a day later. At some point, my mother meets his brother, who confides the family's concern about my father's imminent return to Korea. "If you could just do something to keep him here…" his brother says.

It's not that my mother isn't in love with him. She is. But she is so frequently in love that she's uncertain how long she can expect it to last. Still, she considers his prospects. He's good-looking, clean, a good dancer—and she believes a woman who marries an accountant will always be materially well off. On the strength of these thoughts, she decides to encourage him.

I imagine them, on the way home, after a dance. I see them, in the light of a full moon, as they drive down by the Detroit River. He thinks of the Korean moon, *Taeborum*, the first full moon of the lunar year, and how he and the woman he loved had climbed a hill and made a wish. In the darkness and the quiet of the evening, he can almost imagine he is back in the village where she, his Korean wife, lives. A village forbidden to him as a soldier, but one he was willing to risk his life to visit. My mother slides close to him and before they kiss, he is aware of the sound of the river. It is soothing and familiar. It flows along, never veering from its established course, brushing the boundaries of its perpendicular expanse, rushing forward into a certain future, and if he half-closes his eyes and looks out into the moonlit water, he can almost see before him shoots of rice, rising like sharp blades from iridescent pastures.

SHADOWS

IT IS A BRIGHT YELLOW DAFFODIL DAY, and I make my entrance. There is nothing spectacular about my arrival. My mother, like ninety-six per cent of women who have babies in North America in 1960, opts for the conventional hospital birth. This includes perineal shaving, enema, and epidural anaesthesia. Dead from the waist down, she can't feel my passage or the straight incision the doctor makes in her flesh to allow the gleaming forceps to clamp down on my head. I am healthy, seven pounds four ounces, in spite of the fact my mother smoked the entire term of her pregnancy. In the year that I'm born, Congress has not yet passed the act requiring cigarette labelling, and there are no health warnings on cigarette packages. The US Surgeon General hasn't yet announced smoking as a major cause of lung cancer, and it will be twenty-four years before the rotating cautions on packaging includes "Smoking by pregnant women may result in fetal injury."

I am whisked away, swaddled in pink flannel, and tucked into a hospital nursery crib far from my mother's ward. In future years, irreversible brain damage and mental retardation will be linked to the lead-based paints that coat baby cribs. A decade from now, ninety per cent of children under the age of six will have elevated lead levels in their blood and the government will ban the use of lead-based house paints. Studies will show that newborns who do not bond with their mothers in the sensitive period after birth risk emotional despondency and insecurity. But right now, as a nurse prepares my first bottle and my mother, still numb, prepares to light a cigarette, the daffodil sun is still shining and we are all blithely ignorant.

As a child born in this year, there will forever be things I have missed. I will never get to meet the queen of etiquette, Emily Post, nor watch an original episode of *Howdy Doody*. And, although I will see it in re-run over a hundred times, I will miss witnessing the first televised presidential debate, where Nixon's flop sweat reinforced his title "Tricky Dick" and loses him the election. I will not know the anxiety the world feels when Captain Gary Powers's U-2 spy plane is shot down over Russia or hear the resounding thump of Khrushchev banging his heavy shoe. I will not know what the word *integration* means, or even how to say it for two years, although in this year of my birth, two white public schools in New Orleans will integrate, and in Greensboro, North Carolina, blacks will stage an anti-discrimination sit-in at a lunch counter. Many things that have occurred and are occurring, things that will blossom and flower, go to seed, and blossom again, are both behind and ahead of me.

I will not recall the move my family makes from American Street in Detroit, Michigan, to Ravine Drive in Cleveland, Ohio. I have not yet heard the word *communism*, and would have believed The Bay of Pigs was a place out of Wonderland. I am vaguely conscious of hearing my mother speak to someone about a Berlin Wall, and see it in my mind's eye as the barred panels of my crib. One day I stick my head through the crib's slats and get stuck. I scream but no one comes. As I panic, trying to pull myself free, for the first time in my life I am aware of a terror that my life may end. I am not aware that John F. Kennedy advises "prudent" families to have bomb shelters, that nuclear annihilation may be just around the corner. Some older, calmer part of me takes control, and I twist, then slide, my head back into the crib and fall asleep exhausted. If I dream, I do not recall. If I wake again, I do not remember.

In months to come, I will learn what a yo-yo is, and watch two teenaged girls who live on our block manoeuvre a hula hoop. I will know my mother's favourite soap operas, *The Edge of Night, As the World Turns,* and *Guiding Light.* I'll find comfort in the constant drone of the television. My mother will tell me one Easter that she never liked our house in Detroit because a child died there after eating toadstools. My grandmother will continue to own the house and return to it monthly to collect rent from an impoverished black family. I will not know the word *slum,* but will think when I hear it that it's something good to drink. I will become addicted to the tea and sugar my mother gives me in my glass bottle and develop headaches and become cranky when I don't get it. I will acquire both a terror of darkness and a security blanket, and become an insomniac by the age of three.

Ernest Hemingway will kill himself, Marilyn Monroe will kill herself, William Faulkner will die of a coronary occlusion after years of hard drinking and domestic strife. I will be oblivious to all this. I will be oblivious to the fact that both Aldous Huxley and C. S. Lewis die the same day that Kennedy is assassinated in Texas, and that a week from this day, in England, The Beatles will release their single "I Want to Hold Your Hand."

But I will be aware of the frightening phone call my mother makes, the call in which I still remember hearing her say, "Someone has shot the president." And me, asking, afterwards, "Why? Why did they shoot it?" And my mother saying, still anxious, "Little pitchers have big ears," and my thinking of Dumbo, the flying elephant, and hoping my ears had grown large so I might fly away.

I will remember watching The Beatles on *The Ed Sullivan Show* and seeing thousands of teenaged girls crying and screaming and clinging to a barricade. At four years old, I will feel Beatlemania course through my body, and I will run to the television to kiss Paul McCartney's black-and-white face. My mother will tell me to calm down, and I will ignore her. I will jump on the couch, jump on the chair, and scream like the girls on the TV. I will not remember having seen Topo Gigio or Lamb Chop that evening. I will not remember if they had come before or after, but I will remember the spanking, the stinging flesh, the humiliation. I will remember being dragged down the hallway to my bedroom. I will remember the silence I am left with when my mother closes the door.

I will not know that Valium makes its laboratory debut, nor that Martin Luther King Jr. has a dream. I will not know what the feminine mystique is or why 2.3 million American women find it necessary to use birth control pills. I will only know that the shadow bobbing up and down on my bedroom wall does not belong to the tree branch outside my window but to an evil creature with a prickly face. I will hide, sweating, under my security blanket and almost suffocate.

I will not know my father, an accountant with the New York Central Railroad, who travels constantly and makes infrequent appearances in my life, but I will recall the first Barbie doll he gives me on Christmas Day 1964. She will have a red bubble cut and be wearing a seasonably inappropriate zebra stripe bathing suit and stiletto-heeled sandals. She will smell of new plastic, a smell I will forever identify with Christmas. I will take her swimming suit off and put it back on. I will take her sandals off and put them back on. I will take her head off and put it back on. One spring day when we go on an outing to the "emerald necklace" of Metropolitan Park, I will lose Barbie's head in the Chagrin River. I will be told the current will carry it out to Lake Erie. For the first time in my conscious life, I will pray. The God I pray to is the one who appears on the cover of

my mother's *My Fair Lady* record album. He is manipulating Rex
Harrison's puppet strings, who in turn is manipulating Julie
Andrews's puppet strings. I will make a deal with this God: if he
returns Barbie's head to me, I will never be naughty again. *The Sound
of Music* will not be released until 1965 and the Hayley Mills' movie
The Trouble with Angels not until the following year; *The Flying Nun*
won't be broadcast until 1967. Therefore, I will not know I might
have more bargaining power if I promise God I will become a nun.
Still, miraculously, Barbie's head will appear under a weed on the
bank of the Chagrin. I will thank God and try to make good on our
bargain, but that evening I will not be able to bring myself to eat the
ugly mushy peas on my dinner plate, and will be sent to bed early,
full of guilt, and without apple pie.

Over the years, I will acquire great numbers of Barbie dolls. I will
create elaborate houses for them from boxes, make dishes and
furniture for them from playdough, and even build an amusement
park for them using scraps of wood and nails from the workshop in
our basement. I will rush home from school each day to play with
them and quell my nightly phobias by planning their days. My
Barbie dolls live in a place untainted by the world. Their concerns
are personal, and for the most part, superficial. What should they
wear to go shopping? Should they travel to Tahiti or Rome? Should
they go swimming or skiing?

In Barbie's world, no man has yet orbited the earth; it will be over
twenty years before Barbie herself dons a NASA spacesuit, becomes
an astronaut, and takes to the heavens. And WAR is only a card game
Barbie plays with her best friend, Midge. They will play with a
miniature card deck I get from a penny gumball machine and won't
have a clue about "flamethrowers" or "pineapple bombs," though G.I.
Joe, "fighting man from head to toe," battles into being in 1963 and
will appear in the Barbie carrying cases of a number of my school
friends. My friends will all claim the doll belongs to their brothers,

that they have absconded with it because G.I. Joe is much more handsome than Ken. I will agree with them and feel disloyal until I remove G.I. Joe's clothes and see the crude joints of his naked body.

Sometimes I will watch children's programs when I play with my Barbies. I will watch Captain Kangaroo and Captain Penny. I will like Dancing Bear and be upset that the evil character on *The Bullwinkle Show*, Boris Badenov, and my father share a first name. I will identify with Shrinking Violet in *The Funny Company*, and think Yogi Bear's sidekick, Boo-Boo, would make a great friend. In years to come, I will live in Canada, but the Mountie Dudley Do-Right will do nothing for me.

My favourite programs will all be dark and magical. I will love *The Addams Family*, *The Munsters*, and *Bewitched*. When the soap opera *Dark Shadows* begins in 1966, I will become a devotee. I will have a blouse and a plastic cameo brooch like Angelique's, and before Halloween of 1968, I will find fangs made of chewing wax and become the first female vampire at my grade school.

Over the years, men will relinquish their crewcut hairstyles and women will unravel their bouffants. My mother's hemline will grow shorter and girls at my grade school will be allowed to wear pantsuits instead of dresses. I will have a friend called Rosemary. We will wear identical pantsuits and whisper to each other during atomic bomb drills. Sometimes we will play at her house. Her older brother, John, on whom I will develop a crush, will ride me home on his bike's handlebars. None of us will ever have seen a bike helmet, though in thirty-five years the law will require them for all minors. Both Rosemary and I will have white go-go boots. We will both know how to dance the Pony, but Rosemary is Catholic, so unlike me she will be able to contemplate a brief career as a nun, before deciding on her true vocation as go-go dancer and wife of Monkee Davey Jones. We will fight bitterly over the prospects of my religious conversion to Catholicism, which Rosemary will inform me is simply impossible.

For over a year, I will not see or speak to her, and we will matriculate into different classes, and then one day, during a school assembly celebrating freedom, Rosemary will be on stage, modelling an elegant, silk *ao dai* that her brother John, now a seventeen-year-old soldier, has sent her from Vietnam. I know only vaguely about the war and wonder if Mattel will ever create an *ao dai* for Barbie. I will not have seen the famous photograph of nine-year-old Kim Phuc running naked from a napalm strike, nor will it ever cross my mind that children younger than myself are being maimed and murdered, turned to ash and blown away like dust. I won't know that two million Americans will take part in the war before it ends, that over fifty-eight thousand will be killed, that chemicals made by the same companies to keep our ovens and toilets squeaky clean will be used to defoliate Vietnamese rainforests, and that the effects of these chemicals on human life, in the way of birth defects and cancers, will persist over time.

It is a bright yellow daffodil day, and Rosemary will place her right hand over her heart before she pledges allegiance to the flag. We will speak together again and play in the front yard of her house with our Barbies, scarcely noticing when the chaplain from the army comes to tell her parents why John won't be returning home.

SUPERMAN

MORE POWERFUL THAN A LOCOMOTIVE, able to leap tall buildings in a single bound...

Sometimes, I catch sight of him from the hall, hurtling through the kitchen, soaring past the living room door. No crimson cape. No midnight-blue leotard. The only evidence of his super secret is the handkerchief, monogrammed *S*, tucked inside his suit pocket. Everyone thinks it stands for the first initial of our last name. But it wouldn't take a genius to figure it out: horn-rimmed glasses, black fedora, wing-tipped shoes.

He's dropped the "Clark Kent," left the *Daily Planet*, married my mother instead of Lois Lane. The same month he got the job at the New York Central Railroad as an accountant, the last episode of *The Adventures of Superman* aired, and the railroad's owner, R.R. Young, in the billiard room of his Florida mansion, put a double-barrel shotgun to his head and pulled the trigger. But "the man of steel," a.k.a. my father, with sharp graphite pencils and neat chequered ledger pads, has come to save the day. In his super state, "with powers and abilities far beyond those of mortal men," not only can he "change the course of mighty rivers," but he can bend the books with his bare hands. Though he's supposedly on business trips, I imagine his real adventures: purging the earth of underworld villains, unlacing their victims from ribbons of railways, and once peace is restored, taking off into the stratosphere.

His first earthly home, the farm in Smallville, Kansas, has relocated to a neighbourhood that will become part of Windsor, Ontario, and his folksy, adopted parents, Ma and Pa Kent, have morphed into Momo and Popo, immigrants from the Ukraine and Russia, who came to Canada hoping for a better life. Like the constantly toiling Kents, Elanka and Danielko have, without so much as a corny kernel of all-American rhetoric, instilled in their super-son an ironclad work ethic and an unassailable social conscience.

He exercises these as an adolescent and, then, as a young man working first as a farm labourer and later as a bellhop at the Norton Palmer hotel. He finds his work ethic opens doors for him, while his social conscience shuts them. Still, it's the second he favours and in 1945, a month after two atom bombs are dropped on Japan, my father, though he's not employed there, joins the unionized workers at Ford Motor Company in their historic strike. He thinks the demands are reasonable, particularly the necessity of keeping the union strong. He joins because his father once worked at Dominion Forge—a company that produced steel for the automotive industry at a time when employees weren't allowed to take breaks or go to the bathroom, and English-speaking foremen made slaves of non-English-speaking men: "Mow my lawn, whitewash my fence, shine my shoes." It had nothing to do with the job, but if they refused, they'd get sacked.

So my father commandeers cars and trucks, parks coupes and sedans five across Ford's entranceway, and lets the air out of all of their tires. He does this in orchestration with others, a ubiquitous ballet, in which a blockade is created to prevent police from entering the plant. Men in broad-shouldered overcoats and ivy caps surround him. He's aware things might get ugly and, like any good superhero, is prepared for the fight. If he's arrested and sent to prison, "So be it," he tells himself. If he's beaten and injured, that's just the risk he'll have to take. Sometimes in the name of justice, you put your life on the line. Sometimes, you make sacrifices for a better world. But things don't get ugly, don't get out of hand, even though the police try to force their way through, and my father, with his newfound friends, forces them back. It's only a shoving match, and only one or two people get bruised. The mood is festive. A band arrives and begins to play. People drink lemonade and savour the disobedience. "Look up in the sky, it's a bird, it's a plane…" I imagine all the happy people singing, as my father soars away.

You'd never know to look at him that he's anything but normal— in his Clark Kent attire, he doesn't even draw a glance. No one would suspect his alien origins or believe, for a second, that his first earthly dwelling was one Elanka and Danielko built on Droulliard Road. No trace in his speaking voice of Kryptonese or the Russian/Ukrainian amalgam that Momo and Popo speak at home. But place him in the vicinity of immigrants and his super-susceptibilities begin to show, for no matter what they say, the son of Krypton hears his parents' struggles and feels the radioactive presence of a lost and shattered world. Paralyzed with compassion, neutralized by grief, there are few lead walls to keep our hero from these ravages.

He idolizes his parents, calls them "saints"; when he's been drinking, he declares there's no one in the cosmos who can hold a candle to them. His x-ray eyes grow moist with memories as he recalls Popo's infinite patience and Momo's unconditional love, and how the one and only time he played hooky from school, because a gang of British boys from Walkerville called him "Hunkie" and threatened to hang him from a tree, neither of his parents hit him.

He couldn't bring himself to shame them by telling what had happened, so he lied instead and said he hadn't done his homework. He was surprised that his father lowered his head, seeming every bit as disgraced as if he'd heard the truth, and he was anxious that his mother, who'd been making cabbage rolls and borscht in the kitchen, didn't say a word, but simply wiped the palms of her hands on the dark fabric of her skirt.

He knew his father's story well enough, a peasant boy who ran away from home when he was called for military service. His family couldn't afford a Cossack's uniform, a sabre, or a saddle. They couldn't spare a horse because they didn't have one. He ran, though he had no shoes, and only a rag to wrap over his back. He ran, feeling the lightness of his undernourished body that had known only bread for food the day before, and the vodka that still warmed him. His parents told him he had to go, said if he didn't, they all were doomed, and so he went, through the field towards the churchyard, where he spoke to his sister Paligia in her grave. How he'd loved her when she lived. No earthly shadow had ever marred her smile. "Little mother" is what he called her, and held her tightly, even after her breath subsided and death claimed her as a bride. Now, he was saying goodbye at last, knowing he'd never speak to her again, and wishing so much to join her in the quiet grass. The priest blessed him before he left, and when he came to the outskirts of the village, he stooped and collected a handful of soil—soil he intended to take to his own grave.

Uncertain which direction to take, he held a finger to the sky and allowed the wind to guide him. He expected to collapse, to be abducted by the nomads from the mountains who were said to eat human flesh, or the skinny wolves who howled at night like a choir of demons from hell. But an angel travelled with him for the next three years. He found work enough to eat, and eventually, enough to pay for his passage to Canada. The voyage from Batum to Montreal was gruelling. Many died and were buried at sea. He contracted typhus and almost died himself, but recovered enough to stand and walk from the ship. The sun was shining, and everything felt fluid and unstable. His eyes, sensitive with fever, saw glowing halos around every building and shimmering light on each motor car that sputtered past. Still unsteady on his feet, he swayed like a drunken man as he walked, searching for a boarding house, and the next thing he knew, he was in a muddy ditch, it was night time, and his head was throbbing like a horse's heart. It hurt to move and so he didn't, but tried instead to remember what had happened. There were sounds around him: people's voices, cars, the banging of a door. He tried to lift his right arm, but it wouldn't obey him. Orange pinwheels of pain spun in his head. Slowly, he moved his left arm. He reached toward his chest and inside his shirt searched in vain for the handkerchief-pouch of money that he'd pinned there. The next thing he recalled was the pinkness of the morning and the violent shivering of his body. His clothes were sodden and he thought for a moment that a wave had washed him overboard, until he remembered he was no longer at sea.

The policeman who finally picked him up wasn't kind, nor were the doctors and nurses at the hospital where he was taken. They called him "ignorant foreigner" because he couldn't speak French or English—because he didn't have the foresight to realize that Canada was different from the country he'd left. He was so filthy that a young nurse refused to bathe him. Others refused to examine him until he'd been bathed; and then, finally, grudgingly, they touched his flesh, listened to his heart, took his temperature, all of this with a hate so palpable it felt like a knife blade in his veins.

When Popo told his story, he always mentioned this: while his first experience of Canada was of being beaten, robbed, and left for dead, the thugs who jumped him had injured him less than the doctors and nurses at that hospital. If Super-son had only been present, with his good English and greater understanding of Canada's workings, he'd never have allowed anyone to treat his father that way.

"If you go to school, you have a chance to be more," Popo said. "You have a chance to make us all more. Who will look after us when

I'm too old to work if you don't go to school? Who will look after Momo when I die?" Super-son cried and promised he'd never play hooky again, but Popo continued with the lecture, just as if invisibility were one of the powers that Super-son possessed.

At school, Super-son does well. He's a diligent reader, and his teachers are astounded that foreign illiterates could produce such a boy. Since first learning the letters of the English alphabet and discovering the magic of its meaningful mixtures, Momo and Popo depend on him to decipher all its cryptic combinations: he translates labels at the grocery store, labours over letters from the government, and every night, before he goes to bed, reads the newspaper aloud to his parents, whose rapt attention never falters, even when he stumbles over large and unfamiliar words.

He likes the human interest stories, stories of Irish terriers saving puppies who've been hit by cars, destitute widows discovering fortunes in mattresses, freaks of nature like the Dionne quints. He also relishes the macabre. He follows the story of "The Human Cobra," Vienna's Martha Marek, who conspired with her husband to chop off his leg for insurance money, and then, on her own initiative, poisoned him, their baby daughter, an aunt, and a lodger. He reads out the lurid details slowly, breaking frequently to translate for Momo and Popo the things they don't understand. They click their tongues and shake their heads, just as engrossed in the horror as he is. He tries to explain, in their shared language, that Hitler will bring back the guillotine. "Guillotine?" Momo asks. He mimes a blade falling down on his neck. "Chop!" he shouts. Momo's face goes white.

He reads about the deaths of the notorious bank robbers John Dillinger, Clyde Barrow, and Bonnie Parker, and is fascinated by the story of Canadian gangster Norman "Red" Ryan, who got paroled from Kingston Penitentiary after fooling everyone into believing he'd reformed. He reads about the "Canadian Club Girl," Ella Walker, granddaughter of Hiram, who'd been wed twice, then just like in a fairy story, met and married a prince, and about the rich, wife-seeking bachelor Reginald McLeod, who got the mayor of Windsor to turn City Hall into a sorting place for photographs and correspondence from women eager to be his bride.

Sometimes there are stories about children his own age who have been beaten and abused by their parents. He can never bring himself to feel sympathy for them; he only wonders what they did to deserve it, but when he reads about immigrants like his father whose homes are raided by police for bootleg alcohol and gaming tables, his heart quickens with grief. He knows his parents make vodka; that they sell it to make ends meet.

He also knows that his father despised R.B. Bennett when he was prime minister, and still lionizes Tim Buck, the leader of the Communist Party of Canada, whom the government threw into prison and then tried to have murdered. Super-son fears for Popo. If Popo'd been born in Canada, he could risk supporting communists, but because he comes from Russia, such opinions are dangerous. There are editorials in the paper that decry "complaining immigrants", and say they should all be shipped back to their homelands. His biggest fear is that one day a policeman who hates foreigners will come and arrest Popo for treason and that he, Super-son, will be powerless to stop it.

On the one hand, he wishes he could make Popo think a different way; on the other, he believes that Popo's opinions are true. As Super-son, he's proud of his parents, the way they cope in these hard times, that they're not on relief like most of their neighbours, even though Popo's been laid off from Dominion Forge for two years. But in his identity as the young, ordinary boy Clark Kent, he feels something less comfortable—something sick-making, like shame.

He skips the editorial pages that condemn "unpatriotic immigrants" and turns instead to something light and uplifting: a funny interview with the French-Canadian actress Fifi D'Orsay, a story about a child who miraculously recovers from a rare and incurable disease. He favours the feature called "Scott's Scrap Book" with its cartoon graphics and weird facts. Here, he learns of the existence of a book, *The Trial of William Corder*, bound in the murderer's flesh. He also learns that rabbits' ears point backwards; that General Wrangle, a white Russian, issued his own stamp, and that eighteenth-century toys were once designed to house living birds.

Rarely, there are pieces about scientific breakthroughs and outer space, yet these are the kinds of stories he likes the very best. He reads about the discovery of the asteroid Hermes and how it came perilously close to earth—"Just a mountain loose in the sky" is how the article described it. The thought that such peculiar and potentially cataclysmic entities can suddenly materialize out of nowhere exhilarates him, and he often finds himself thinking about the vast universe and what mysteries exist there.

Under his bedcovers at night when he should be sleeping, he reads by flashlight *The Time Machine, The Island of Dr. Moreau, A Journey to the Centre of the Earth*. He gets these books and many others from the public library, even though, during these hard times, it has been forced to shut down branches and reduce its hours. He also gets hold of pulp magazines, though some cost as much as a quarter, and some are forbidden because they have naked women on their covers.

Super-son reads well into the early hours of each morning, always ready to switch off the flashlight if he should hear stirrings beyond his door. Even though with his super senses he can hear sounds over great distances and at many frequencies, he gets so absorbed in his readings that Momo inevitably catches him. She takes his books and flashlight away, laments his stupidity and disobedience, and insists it's this habit of his that's responsible for his nearsightedness, which costs her and Popo so much money each year in eye examinations and new glasses of increasing strength. He endures her lecture, feels guilty for a time, but this doesn't prevent him, the very next day, from hunting in her room for the contraband, from stealing it back, and proceeding with his reading, just as if she'd never said a word. It's a game they play—her authentic rebuke, his authentic contrition, night after night after night, until things inevitably change.

The same year that Momo and Popo finally lose the house on Drouillard because they can't pay their property taxes, and move to a tiny shack on Francois Road, Superman appears for the first time on the cover of *Action Comics*. He's lifting an automobile, smashing it against a rock, while three frazzled villains, who had abducted Lois, run for their lives.

Super-son loves this comic and reads it several times. He reads it under the sheets in his new bedroom, a bedroom which Popo has fashioned in the attic and is slightly larger than a closet. Because the house is cardboard-thin, even when Super-son is captivated by his red-caped hero, he can hear each whisper and footfall on the floor below. He can hear the neighbours fighting and a train's whistle, which, though thirty miles away, shakes the flimsy roof.

He doesn't know what genius has created this "physical marvel who has sworn to devote his existence to those in need," but immediately experiences a sense of kinship. Perhaps in some parallel universe, he already realizes this is who he'll become.

Is it a coincidence that Jerry Siegel and Joe Shuster, creators of this "champion of the oppressed," are the sons of immigrant fathers, too? Siegel's father, a struggling immigrant from Lithuania, was murdered by robbers who broke into his store. Shuster's father, an impoverished immigrant from the Netherlands, moved his family from place to place in Toronto before finally leaving to look for work in Ohio. It was here, in Cleveland, in one of the city's high schools, where the two boys met. Did they ever speak about their feelings of helplessness? Did they, like Super-son, both wish and fail to protect their foreign fathers? I wonder if Super-son ever pondered such thoughts, though I know his curiosity doesn't extend in these directions. He is more likely to consider the probability of life on other planets and wonder how it is that entire worlds can crumble, leaving nothing in their wake.

Four months after Superman's debut, a Polish neighbour who barters bread and headcheese for vodka will arrive at the door on Francois Street, screaming that there has been an "inwazja."

"Martians from outer space," he'll sob in English, before reflexively lapsing back into his mother tongue. Momo will rush to the kitchen for a shot glass and whisky to help him deal with his shock. Popo will try to calm him. Super-son will turn on the big wooden radio in the corner and listen.

He thinks the Polish man is drunk and delusional. He can't believe his ears when a Professor Pierson from Princeton University talks about the destructive capabilities of these hostile aliens that have, apparently, landed in New Jersey. He feels a buzz in his head, a kind of lightness that makes his body incredibly heavy. A news announcer interrupts with a bulletin. The state militia has declared martial law. Super-son knows, from looking at maps, that New Jersey is not all that far away. He wonders if there's some way he can get there. If there's something he can do to help. Then, instantly aware that the room has fallen silent, that Momo and Popo and the Polish man are all listening to this broadcast, his call to action rapidly shifts. His driving objective becomes one of stopping it, of pulling the plug or skewing the dial, of sparing his parents from this cataclysmic terror. But Popo isn't acting terrified. In fact, he's laughing, and Super-son wonders if panic has driven him mad.

"It's a joke," Popo chuckles, pouring the neighbour a second shot. "You can hear. Listen!" Both the Polish man and Momo strain to listen. Super-son listens more closely too, but doesn't hear anything that would lead him to believe it's not true.

Later, once Orson Welles confesses the hoax, Popo explains to Super-son that the tone of Welles's voice gave it away. If such an awful thing were truly happening, there would have been a quality in his voice that Popo would have detected. Super-son is embarrassed that he was unable to perceive the deception. He's embarrassed that he was taken in. He wants Popo to teach him how to know better in the future, but Popo can't teach him this. It's a matter of experience, Popo tells him. It's a matter of having to listen extra closely and not hear the meaning of any of the words at all.

In 1952, when he is twenty-five years old, Super-son prepares to leave his parents' house on Francois Road and join the US Army to help end the bloody and expensive war in Korea. Strategically, as a defender of truth, justice, and now, of course, of the American way, fighting communists is the best thing he can think to do. On a practical level, it will give him work and entitle him to a free education at the Detroit Institute of Technology, just across the river. On an emotional level, it will help shield his Russian father from increasing accusations of communist sedition.

Famous people, like Arthur Koestler and Richard Wright, who were communists in the thirties, have not only denounced their former affiliations with the party, but have become vociferous opponents. They claim they were ignorant; that they got sucked in by the promise of a better world; that they didn't know the truth at first.

Super-son explains all this to Popo, hoping it will have some impact, but Popo sits stony-faced, not saying a word. Momo mops tears from her cheeks and neck with a square of cloth that usually covers a hole in the arm of her chair. Even though Super-son knows that leaving his parents will be the most agonizing thing he's ever done, he dons a combat uniform and takes flight.

In my mind's eye, I see him sailing over oceans, not in khaki but in the S-man's characteristic red and blue, the very same shades and colours that inhabit the Taegeuk, a circle at the centre of the South Korean flag. He arrives to the sound of cheers and applause, for every South Korean present knows he's come to save them. He feeds the orphans with his own rations, builds tents for the newly homeless, protects the honour of young maiden refugees, and yet still has time to engage in battle.

No need for bulky headgear or the flak jackets that claim to deflect sixty-five per cent of shells. He thrusts his chest forward, bends the barrels of antagonistic guns. "Take that, you scoundrels!" he shouts, as squads of frightened enemies retreat.

I never imagine the misty hills erupting like volcanoes or the parachutes falling like mushrooms from the sky. I don't see or smell the bright flashes of mortar, the way the trees buck when a cannon fires, or how half-frozen men, huddled in their trenches, get blown to kingdom come. In my fantasy, the landscape where my father walks looks nothing like a grey and cratered moon, and the majority of North Korean enemies he's fighting are tough and strong and bad, not a bunch of hungry rice farmers who became soldiers because they were promised more and better food.

I don't know that this conflict is sometimes called "the unnecessary war" and in years to come will be called "the forgotten war;" that it consisted of daily skirmishes of gaining and losing the same ground, of winning and then surrendering the same scorched and defoliated dirt hills again and again.

For now, the S-man blazes to the rescue, full of justice and conviction and an overwhelming impulse to do good in the world. Little does he know the real dangers that surround him, which have nothing to do with showers of bullets and exploding bombs. His Achilles heel will be all the hard-working, non-English-speaking labourers who inhabit both the North and South of this land. His super-strengths diminish and he weakens. He'll wonder what he's doing here. The questions descend and fester: What if his father had stayed in Russia? Would he be fighting the ally instead of the enemy?

Long after my father is dead, writer Mark Miller will imagine what the world might be like if Superman had grown up in the USSR, and will create the three-part miniseries *Superman: Red Son* for DC comics. This Soviet incarnation of the man of steel whose rocket lands on a collective farm in the Ukraine will stand for international socialism, Stalinism, and the Five-Year Plan. He will wear a hammer and sickle on his chest, instead of an *S*, and his mild-mannered Clark Kent persona will work for *Pravda*, instead of the *Daily Planet*. But just like the idealistic hero that we know, this alien alien wants only to help mankind. He truly believes the values he promotes will make the world a better place. Like the capitalist son of Krypton, the communist one is equally naive, seeing his way as the only way and his convictions as the only proper points of view—a benevolent mask, some would suggest, disguising an unconscious despot.

My father sobs like a baby when he hears from Francois Road. His parents have asked a neighbour to write the letter. "Your father is sick and your mother is beside herself with worry. Is there any way you can come back home?"

Popo is suffering from leg pain. His foot and ankle have turned the colour of porcelain. Momo tried to make him go to the doctor, but he insisted he was fine; now, he can't walk.

Super-son finagles leave. He takes Popo to a specialist, where he's diagnosed with peripheral vascular disease. He needs medication, maybe surgery, and has sternly been told he must stop smoking. Since 1935, medical studies have shown smoking decreases blood circulation, but reports on the health dangers of this phenomenon have been downplayed in the popular press. In the local Windsor paper, cigarette smoking is said to be unhealthy only to some individuals, and Doctor

White from Boston, considered an authority on the subject, asserts, "We don't think tobacco causes disease."

The memory of articles such as these, which Super-son once read aloud, fuels Popo's resistance. He doesn't trust doctors and even though he can't walk, he isn't convinced he's really sick. Super-son asks questions and translates the doctor's answers in a fashion his parents understand.

For the rest of his life, no matter where he travels, no matter what he's doing, Super-son, when summoned, will return to Momo and Popo faster than a speeding bullet. When Popo is admitted to Hôtel-Dieu hospital, although Super-son's first civilian job in Europe pays well and has great potential for advancement, without hesitation or any consideration for his wife and two infant sons, he will don his S-man persona, give immediate notice, and fly back home. It costs him the earth, but he removes his father from Windsor and admits him to Detroit's Henry Ford Hospital, where vascular surgery is a specialty. There, doctors take a vein from Popo's chest and use it to bypass a section of artery in his leg, but Popo says he's a busy man and instead of resting, as soon as he returns home, climbs a ladder to patch a hole in the roof and destroys the bypass. He stoically endures the pain until his toe turns black, at which time Super-son is called, once again, to save the day.

But he cannot save Popo's leg, which must be amputated, nor can he ultimately stop the progression of gangrene, which moves like the forces of evil in the world, and which Popo attempts to contain by self-deception. Heartache corrodes the man of steel, makes him buckle like a soft piece of cheese, imprints like an asteroid on his memory that ill-fated date of his father's death, which also happens to be his wife's thirtieth birthday. For now and forever there will be no joy on this unholy day, only sombre reflection and rage. Even if he'd witnessed the destruction of Krypton, his suffering could not be more profound.

Popo is interred in the mausoleum at Greenlawn Memorial Gardens, which is large and full of white marble and smells like gladiolus flowers and sour milk. Momo holds tearful vigils there while Super-son, in their shared language, calls to Popo in his tomb.

Though alcohol is said to have no effect on the last son of Krypton, there is a cocktail called "The Drunken Superman" that consists of tequila, triple sec, and 151- proof rum, and while he never consumes this potion, he frequently imbibes the more mundane manhattan, screwdriver, and martini. He drowns his sorrows for months after Popo dies, then manically celebrates when he gets the accounting job at the railroad. After he's transferred to Chicago, he spends a lot of time drinking in the lounge at O'Hare Airport. One late snowy night, when his flight to New York is long delayed and he's been super-slurring to strangers about his parents' sainthood, he gets into a brawl with a couple of men who have insulted him. He believes he's fighting for truth and justice, for the honour of Momo and the memory of Popo, for the respect of all the hard-working immigrants who've ever been looked down upon, insulted, and abused.

He doesn't make it to a phone booth. He doesn't change into his super-wear. The police, not realizing who he is, throw him into the drunk tank. He misses his meeting in New York and arrives home early the next morning, limping. His Clark Kent glasses are busted at the nose, his fedora crumpled, his monogrammed handkerchief wrapped around a wounded hand. Dry blood crusts his chin and cheek, and the moment I see him, I feel the world begin to crack, and know with an irrevocable certainty that he will never fly again.

INTERCOURSE

BEFORE I STARTED SCHOOL, when my mother was overweight but not yet obese, she took some pains with her appearance: filing and painting her nails, curling her hair with spiky rollers and long pink pins, then putting a plastic hairdryer cap over her head. It was a portable hairdryer that sounded like a vacuum cleaner and drowned out the dialogue of her soap operas. The word *diet* was perpetually on her lips, and I recall the assortment of diet foods she ate—meal replacement milkshakes, chocolate bars, and cookies—and how I coveted them. All morning long she would busy herself with housework; I recall the baskets full of my father's white shirts and handkerchiefs she ironed, and the smell of furniture polish she rubbed over the sharp corners of the ugly blond Formica coffee table—a table that grew increasingly chipped and stained over the years, but remained with us throughout our entire existence as a family. Our black-and-white television was on all day, divulging stories of tormented families, of loves gone wrong, of illegitimate pregnancies, adoptions, affairs, and divorce.

"Why's that lady crying?" I'd ask occasionally, looking up from my puzzles or my dolls.

"Because she's going to have a baby," my mother would say, almost harshly, her eyes intent on the screen.

"Is it sad to have a baby?" I'd persist.

"That depends on the baby," she'd say, annoyed at my intrusions, but even so, my curiosity got the better of me and I couldn't stop: "Why's she kissing that man, and not the man she was kissing yesterday?" "Doesn't she love him anymore?" "Why is she kissing him for such a long time?" "How do you give a baby away?"

My mother's angry "Shhhhh!" sounded like her steamy iron pressing down on cotton. "Children should be seen and not heard," she said, and as I grew older and even more inquisitive, this mantra became the hinge of all our conversations. But in my preschool years, when her favourite soap opera, *General Hospital*, came on, she rarely had to check me. I knew when she stopped ironing, collected her needlework, and positioned herself in the Naugahyde armchair that my very breathing could disrupt her focus, and I kept my silence. This focus was not singular, and perhaps that's why it could be so easily disturbed, for all the while she absorbed the emotional nuances of the ill-fated nurse Jessie Brewer and her philandering husband, my mother's fingers worked like an artist's.

Later in the day, when the soaps were over and the house smelled clean and glistened from her labour, she would tend to her sewing again, this time using her machine or pinning frail, transparent pattern pieces on fabric that stretched across the dining room table. Even as a small child, I marvelled at her speed and precision, and when she offered me the chance to pin or cut, I never took it, overawed by her unerring abilities. Most of her sewing projects were clothes for me: dresses, skirts, jumpers, blouses, sunsuits, slacks, coats, robes, pyjamas. There was nothing she could not make, though she chose only to sew clothing she considered "worth the effort." And the effort was exorbitant, since she would add a complex embroidered picture to virtually every item she made. There was a scene with a Dutch boy and girl standing next to a windmill in a field of colourful tulips, which she embroidered onto the full skirt of a blue dress. On the chest of a sleeveless white blouse she recreated a scene from *Mary Poppins*. On a pink jumper she fashioned a watering jug from a rainbow of seam binding, and then filled it with every type of embroidered flower imaginable.

I recall one time when my father, after drinking too much, demanded that she list the costs of her dressmaking. He pulled out a notepad and one of his long, sharp accountant's pencils and began: "Cloth, thread, buttons…" He wrote in small, scrunched angular letters. In another column, he wrote: "Sewing machine, scissors, needles, electricity." He insisted my mother detail every expense. Finally, in a third column, he wrote "Labour." In the early, sloppy stage of his drunkenness, my mother always attempted to humour him, to keep the peace, as she called it. On this occasion, however, he rapidly became bullying.

He insisted on knowing the hours she had put into the dress. "What? Twelve? Fifteen? Twenty?" She didn't answer, but stood from her seat in the dining room. "Let's say for the sake of argument, you only spent nine hours making that dress." Even I, at age five, knew that vastly more than nine hours went into the embroidery on the dress alone.

"How much do you think your labour's worth an hour?" he persisted. My mother was on her way through the kitchen's swinging doors. "Let's just say, a dollar twenty-five an hour. For the sake of argument, we'll keep it at minimum wage."

His pencil scratched the pad in front of him, and I knew my mother was crying in the kitchen. "My God!" he shouted, as if he were genuinely surprised. "That dress cost us a small fortune!" He made me run and get the department store catalogue my mother kept in the magazine rack. He leafed through it until he found the children's section, and then banged his hand so hard on the table that the ice in his drink rattled for several seconds. "Four dollars and ninety-six cents!" he shouted. "That's what it costs to buy a kid's dress! Your labour alone at minimum wage could have bought her two dresses and a couple of pairs of socks."

"You're drunk," I heard her whisper as he entered the kitchen, waving his notepad. "If you want me to go out to work, I will!"

My father's words were slurred now. "No wife of mine is going to work."

"I work all day!" my mother told him. "But I don't get minimum wage."

What my mother seemed incapable of saying, perhaps because she was unaware of it herself, was that she found great satisfaction in creating and that her sewing was the only practical, domestic, conventionally sanctioned way she could sneak for herself a very small bit of creative pleasure.

The argument quickly degenerated into my father's insults about my mother's cooking. Having grown up with food rationing in wartime England, my mother still believed fried eggs and chips were perfectly acceptable dinner fare. She didn't watch Julia Child's cooking show. She distrusted all things "foreign," including the trendy food fashions, which had neighbouring housewives buying fondue pots and scurrying to enroll in French cooking classes.

What my father didn't know and what would surely have caused him to make even more triumphant calculations was the amount of time my mother spent on sewing outfits for my Barbie dolls. She took no less care with these creations than she did with my clothes, adding tiny embellishments—pockets and pleats, collars and cuffs—to the masterful, minuscule garments that looked as if they had been shrunk down from well-made women's wear, instead of tailor-made for miniature human models. Unlike the manufactured doll clothing, there was nothing sloppy in my mother's work. Each seam and hem was sewn with the smallest, tightest stitching imaginable, as if she had used a magnifying glass in the operation. And the outfits she created were magnificent. Dark blue velvet gowns with gold brocade, chiffon pyjamas, fur-lined jackets.

The more attention she gave to this clothing, the more I felt inclined to play with my dolls, and, influenced by the soap operas, I created elaborate romantic adventures for them. One day my mother conceived of having a large wedding for my dolls. Barbie and Ken would be the bride and groom, of course; Midge and Alan, maid of honour and best man; Skipper and Scooter, flower girls; and Ricky, the newest addition to my Barbie group, ring bearer. I'd make the church from a large box and folded sheets of cardboard to create the pews. Mary Ann Richards, a teenaged girl who lived at the end of our street, gave me her old flock-haired Ken doll. He hadn't aged particularly well. He'd be the minister, I decided, and there were a number of other even less impressive dolls who could be wedding guests.

My mother was filled with her own vision, which had less to do with the church ceremony (I already decided it would be disrupted by Ken's old girlfriend, Julia) and more to do with the reception and honeymoon afterwards, for which she'd sew an entire and elaborate trousseau. "We can make a wedding cake out of Styrofoam as well," she said, "and I can get hold of some miniature champagne glasses from the craft store."

For months, the ensuing wedding became our prime focus, as my mother created fashion after fashion, and I set to work building a chapel out of cardboard. The first thing she completed was the wedding dress. She made it in white satin and trimmed it in lace and tiny mother-of-pearl beads. It was as beautiful to touch as it was to look at, and I made sure I kept it well out of my father's way. Then she made a black tuxedo, a white spread-collar shirt, a black bow tie, and a matching cummerbund for Ken and exactly the same for Alan and Ricky. She made Midge's gown out of bright blue taffeta with a pale chiffon overlay and a crinoline underskirt, and Skipper and Scooter were also in taffeta and chiffon, but their dusty-rose and peach dresses were ankle length with beaded satin sashes. Then there were negligees and nightgowns for Barbie as well as a fine bed jacket, casual travel wear, and evening dresses. Ken also got two new suits, one casual, one formal, and some satin pyjamas that matched Barbie's nightclothes. To add to all of this, she created two sets of luggage out of felt and cardboard for the newlyweds.

When the wedding finally took place, I was too excited about the honeymoon and all the adventures the outfits would afford to allow the cheap Julia doll, who wasn't a Barbie anyway, to upset it. The newlywed Ken and Barbie drove off in a limousine (converted from a shoe box) to Niagara Falls (the bathroom) where they stayed at a luxury hotel (a shelf in the bathroom cupboard). When they finally returned to their penthouse apartment in New York (the bookcase in the living room), Barbie was pregnant (I shoved a tiny gumball machine baby under her jersey). I decided she would put it up for adoption. But before Barbie could even give birth, my mother intervened, shrieking that I was a "Filthy-minded little bugger" for having done such a thing, and asking if putting the baby under Barbie's dress was Mary Ann Richards's idea.

At the time, I didn't know why she became so irate, but later I would realize this rage erupted around anything that she construed as sexually percipient. Once, a few years after the Barbie episode, when I was playing dress-up with some old clothes and beads and make-up she'd given me, I stuffed the front of a dress with a pair of hand towels. My brother had once dressed up in this dress and stuffed the chest in a similar way, and it had amused her—but when I did it, it released a torrent: "You dirty little bugger," she shouted, dragging me away from the bathroom mirror. "You filthy, disgusting girl." She slapped me and tore at the chest of the dress. "Using my good hand towels, too!" she screeched. Her demon likewise took possession when I drew a picture of a woman in a low-cut dress and tried to give her some cleavage. She seized the picture, pronounced it "smutty," and tore it to pieces.

As I grew older, my mother often told me stories of her life in England: how she watched bombs fall, became gravely ill, and was always hungry during the war. She started work at fifteen as a shorthand typist, but flitted from job to job since there were many to choose from. As a young woman, she spent most of her time, when not working, at dance halls. She learned to smoke cigarettes and pluck her eyebrows, which made her feel "wicked." She dated many good-looking soldiers, though she could only remember the name of one. His she recalled because of his filthy ears, which killed her infatuation like frost on a rose. "I was in love with love," she'd tell me, and never once suggested that any kind of sexual element might exist to sully the romance.

If it weren't for her soap operas and my associations with girlfriends who were more knowledgeable than me, I would have had no idea how pregnancy occurred, how babies entered the world, or what menstruation was.

I was twelve years old and my mother forty-four when she gave birth to her fourth child. She never told me she was pregnant; it was my brother, her confidant, who did. He said she had considered an abortion, but had dithered too long and now had to go through with it. I was sure he was joking. I couldn't tell she was pregnant because by this time she was grossly overweight. As a consequence, her doctor felt the pregnancy was very risky and eventually admitted her to hospital for a month, putting her on a special diet. Again, it was my brother who imparted this news on the first morning of her absence.

Many years later, when my mother and I were sharing a bottle of wine, she alluded to these times and confessed she could not bring herself to tell me she was pregnant "Because then you'd know what

I'd been up to and you'd think the worse of me." It was an odd declaration, fragile and strangely cropped, like an old pattern piece discovered in the groove of a chair many long years after the search for it had ended.

FOR POSTERITY

MY FATHER'S LARGE HAND contains my small one. I think of them together, a tender white clam curled in a warm, weathered shell. He doesn't often take my hand, but we're at Niagara Falls, boarding the *Maid of the Mist*, and a surge of tourists threatens to separate us in their swell. My brothers have gone ahead without being noticed, and when they gripe that my father is playing favourites, he excuses himself by saying: "She's only a little girl."

He helps me struggle into the bulky black rain poncho I'm given. It's too big for me, and I have trouble lifting my arms. He's brought his camera and he takes a picture. "For posterity," he says, and I wonder who she might be. I envision a woman in a babushka like my grandmother's, a distant relative in Russia I've never seen.

It's 1965 and I'm too young to know that it's not Russia, but the Soviet Union where any unknown relatives might be. I don't know that my country lives in a suspended state of mutual hatred with the country of my ancestors, or that even as the Vietnam War burns, this "Cold War," as it's called, has already shown signs of thawing. From these insulated precincts of youth, I know neither what came before nor what to predict for the future. Who could foresee that in twenty-six years the Union would collapse, or that in twenty-one, a nuclear disaster at Chernobyl would inflict an aggressive form of thyroid cancer on countless children in its surrounding regions?

The world is a foreign body to me. I have no knowledge or feeling for it and don't regard it in any way as my legacy. Instead, I'm concerned with my own physicality—the discomfort of this scratchy poncho; its stink of car tires and fish. When my father finishes with the photo shoot, I stand and try to breathe the air. Tourists surround us. I inhale their stifling anticipation and begin to feel sick. I search the crowd for some diversion and at last find a couple kissing. I imagine that they're newlyweds; that they've come here for their honeymoon. The couple whisper to each other and kiss again. "Honeymoon," I think, and imagine a sticky luminous syrup dripping from the sky.

If I were old enough to read the newspaper, I'd know that the convention bureau here greeted more honeymooners last spring than any other spring on record—that newlyweds from all over North America, and even some from Mexico and Japan, claimed a honeymoon certificate and got a pass for the bride to visit attractions as her husband's guest. But I don't need to know this to think about the importance of marriage to girls, to consider how honeymoons are almost equal to weddings. I escape all of the unpleasantness of my senses simply by thinking of Niagara Falls as a place for love.

There are heart-shaped beds, like boxes of Valentine chocolates, in our hotel. There are heart-shaped ashtrays in the stores, heart-shaped picture frames, heart-shaped postcards. I asked my mother, who decided to shop instead of come with us, if she'd buy me a heart-shaped locket. I thought she might because I know she has a golden one with a picture of her father inside. She said I was too young for jewellery, but I know this is just her way of saying "No."

I watch the couple kissing and try to imagine what being in love is like. Others on the boat watch, too, and the couple seem oblivious. My father nudges me to stop gawking. He tries to distract me by pointing toward the Falls, but I'm captivated by the couple's uninhibited exhibition. I wonder if I should ever fall in love, if I, too, would be so publicly carefree.

Looking back on this day from adulthood and thinking about the innocence and self-absorption of love, I'm aware that in all probability, not only I but likely everyone on that boat was unaware of "Love Canal." It's likely that if someone had told us it existed just east of here, in the United States, we would have imagined a romantic destination, believed it had been named to convey this impression, and never, in a million years, guessed the name was to commemorate the developer, William T. Love.

We'd be intrigued to hear that the mile-long ditch which came to bear his name had originally been intended as a canal to provide cheap electricity to the neighbourhood of "Model City"—a happy, healthy, alcohol-free community he'd envisioned. Problems with financial backing and advances in electrical technology were ultimately what thwarted him, and his property was foreclosed upon and sold in 1910.

Only the jokers on board might chuckle "Love failed!" but few familiar with the slang of prostitution would be able to resist commenting on the next part of the story. Love Canal was eventually purchased as a chemical dumping site by Elon Hooker, the founder of Hooker Chemical. It was filled with some 21,000 tons of hazardous waste, covered over with dirt, and then sold for one dollar to the municipal school board for the construction of the 99th Street Elementary School. Hooker warned the board about the toxic waste; he even tried to prevent them from selling the excess land to real estate developers, but the wheels of progress are rarely slowed by reason.

On the *Maid of the Mist*, as we listen to a pre-recorded tour guide crackling through the boat's speaker system, we're ignorant of the fact that bad smells are vaporizing from the earth at Love Canal; that strange chemical substances are surfacing in the schoolyard and seeping into basements. We don't know that letters have been written, that complaints have been made, and that with the exception of trucking in a few loads of soil and clay as a suppressant, the city has, so far, taken no action. Also unknown to us, of course, is the fact that this toxic waste is insidiously seeping into the Niagara River—that the mist from these cascading falls, which dampens our jackets and infuses our lungs, contains traces of these chemicals.

The local paper, the *Evening Review*, has reported nothing on this. Amid stories of air cadets winning rifle shoots, students winning public speaking contests, and highland dance troupes dancing their way to regional renown, there's no mention of complaining residents of the Love Canal area, and no indication of profound environmental damage in this region.

But there is an article on scuba divers who've unearthed a warehouse of historic treasures: muskets, anchors, parts of ships. They may have found the American gunboat the USS *Detroit*. It got caught in the strong currents of the Niagara River during the War of 1812 and was torched and sunk in battle. There's a thousand-pound cannon they've raised. It's been sandblasted and the city will set it on a model undercarriage so it can serve as a historical showpiece. They've found hundreds of old shoes, an upside-down tugboat, and a mast seat, almost perfectly preserved. They know the past can't just be washed away, but toxic waste and chemicals, unlike historic artifacts, are invisible to the naked eye, and the river's waters are as cold and transparent as a ghost.

Since last December, thousands of dead fish have littered the beaches and shores from Niagara-on-the-Lake to Queenston, and their physical presence that extends in a ten-foot strip for approximately seven miles is a phenomenon too visible and disconcerting to go unreported. Their stench increases by the day, and the Chamber of Commerce fears a loss in tourism, but a representative from the Department of Land and Forests who inspected the area assured those concerned that the smell should dissipate in a week or two.

What's caused this eerie massacre? No one seems to know or care. What's paramount is the costly disposing of the overpowering carcasses, which neither federal, provincial, nor municipal authorities are willing to do.

On the *Maid of the Mist*, we don't see the awesome spectacle of dead fish, but marvel, instead, at the power and majesty of the steaming falls as the crackling voice over the loudspeaker tells us the legend of the beautiful Indian princess, Lelawala, who lived on the shores of the Niagara River and for whom our boat is named. As legend has it, once, long ago, for no apparent reason, members of Lelawala's tribe began dying. To appease the thunder god, Lelawala's father, the tribe's chief, sacrificed his daughter to the Falls. As she tumbled over the misty void, she was swept up by one of the god's sons who had fallen in love with her. Lelawala agreed to marry him after he revealed that a large water snake was poisoning the river and killing her people. In a dream, she conveyed this information to her father, and the tribe was successful in defeating the snake, whose remains we still see as the semicircle at the brink of the Horseshoe Falls.

We all enjoy this romantic legend, without benefit of irony, just as we enjoy the raw and unspoiled manifestations of nature, which the Falls are purported to be. The fact the legend is a white man's fabrication, that human sacrifice was never practised by any of the tribes of the Six Nations, and that in three decades The Maid of the Mist Corporation will stop broadcasting the story because native groups threaten to protest, are particulars we would never want to know. What's important is the way the legend seeps into our shared and unexamined assumptions, the way our minds reflexively accept—

the savagery of native people, the necessity to sacrifice young female life, and "love, love, love," as The Beatles will sing two years from now, because love and marriage and honeymoons are what Niagara Falls is all about.

I push my way to the starboard railing to search the mist. I think if I look hard enough, there's a chance I'll see Lelawala's face rising like a cloud. There are questions I'd like to ask her, like Why, if she saved her people, they don't live here anymore? And is she living happily ever after, like princesses are supposed to, or is she wet and cold and sad beneath these falls?

From all I've ever heard, such a question is preposterous. Lelawala should be joyous having surrendered herself to a god. He will look after her, care for her, make sure that she wants for nothing, yet my question surfaces, a poisoned fish on the river, which I can neither rid myself of nor ignore.

I'm too young to read the local newspaper's advice column by Doris Clark, with the headline "Husband Grows Cold." I could never imagine the plight of the woman who signs herself "Puzzled and Sad" and laments that her husband who once "worshipped the ground she walked on" now stays out late drinking with the boys, flirts with all the pretty girls, and calls her insulting names. The fact a honeymoon can be over, as Doris tells her distressed correspondent, is something that would never have occurred to me. According to Doris, a woman needs to take stock at these times—she needs to ask herself: Has she been nagging? Has she been making life anything less than serene for her man? Has she let her physical appearance go? Love can die and honeymoons end, for any number of reasons.

I don't realize that at Niagara Falls, death and love are inextricably bound. I don't know that a twenty-one-year-old resident, an ex-Vietnam War Marine, brimming with an urge to destroy, recently slid the glistening blade of his foot-long bayonet into the bodies of two young women, then, like a lover, lay on top of one of the corpses, waiting for police to arrive.

I've never seen the movie *Niagara* in which Rose Loomis, played by Marilyn Monroe, brings her depressed, jealous, and volatile husband to the Falls in order to kill him. He, however, gets wind of her plot, kills both her and her young stud of a boyfriend, and then, in a boat that runs out of gas, floats down the Niagara River rapids and commits suicide.

Suicide occurs frequently here, though tourists, enraptured by the romance of the Falls or fixed by the sweet façades of love, would never think so. The city is cagey about revealing statistics. Police, however, have estimated that on average one person per month uses the Falls to do themselves in. The majority of suicides, apparently, jump into the river at the place where the most dramatic currents eddy, just above the Horseshoe Falls. They don't see the hidden concrete dam that diverts water to a hydro plant, and don't know that city employees are contacted whenever jumpers are spotted, so they can shut the dam's gates and reduce the speed of the river's flow.

On the *Maid of the Mist*, we glide closer to the Falls, and the entire deck rumbles. So removed is death from love for me, that at first, I don't even realize that the face I'm seeking in the mist belongs to a ghost. A gust of wind off the Falls glues the black poncho to my body like a straitjacket while a burst of water drenches me. Shivering, I turn to my father and shout above the deafening thunder: "You'd never sacrifice me, would you Dad?" I want him to say more than just "Never." I want him to assure me that he'll take care of me for the rest of my days. I want him to promise that he'll keep me eternally cocooned in this heart-shaped shell of childhood and never allow me to be cast adrift, but my words sink beneath breakers of wind, and I see that he's focused on the couple who have been kissing. The man is now carrying the woman in his arms, just as if he were carrying her across a threshold, and playfully swinging her out over the boat, as she squeals. My father's eyes, spirited with this amusement, remain completely oblivious to the chilling splendour around us, to the past we are leaving and to the future, where we will sail. He is oblivious to the laboured rattle of the boat, and to my brothers who sit in petrified silence, and of my cold and desperate hand that, trembling, recoils from the mist, attempting to grasp for his.

THE CONSTRUCTION OF FRAMES

TWO YEARS BEFORE ANDY WARHOL was shot, my father began bringing home art. Not the kind of art Warhol did—depictions of soup cans, electric chairs, and dollar bills—but the kind of art my father considered "real," paintings done by "the masters," canvases that "had endured the test of time."

With every fill-up of gas, for a quarter my father could purchase such a picture. In the past the station had sold soft-drink glasses and cutlery, and my father, who travelled a great deal, took advantage of these promotions, but not with the same enthusiasm as he embraced the pictures. They were all textured with identical faux brush strokes, printed on inch-thick cardboard, "suitable for framing," the gas station advertised. And my father would bring them home, at first one at a time, but soon in groups of sixes or sevens, as the gas station tried to dispense with pictures no one would buy.

Some weekends my father would build frames for these pictures from scraps of wood he had hanging around. He'd show me how his radial-arm saw worked, though he'd never let me feed the wood in by myself. Sometimes, however, he'd let me choose from an array of baby food jars the suitable group of nails we would use for the frame, and once he got the nails started, he'd let me hammer them in the rest of the way. We worked like this as Tchaikovsky's *Waltz of the Flowers* played in the background. My father subscribed to a classics record club, and when the spirit moved him would call the entire family together for a "musical appreciation" session, which consisted of him playing snippets of symphonies, waltzes, and arias and us all trying to guess the composers' names. It didn't really matter if we appreciated the music or not. The title of his impromptu sessions was misleading—what was important was that we could correctly put a composer's name to a composition. This, my father told us, was an invaluable skill that would astound and impress friends and foes alike—it would make us seem superior in culture and intelligence.

For similar reasons, my father would pay my two brothers and me a nickel for every three-syllable word we used and fifty cents for every poem we could commit to memory and recite with feeling. We didn't have a lot of choice in poetry. Besides my father's war history books and science fiction collection, our bookcases, which my father also built himself, housed numerous volumes of Reader's Digest abridged classics and a complete set of fern-green Funk & Wagnall encyclopedias, but only three volumes of poetry. The one we made the most use of was my father's anthology of *Best Loved Poems*. There were some relatively short poems in this collection with helpful rhyming schemes. My father had promised he'd buy us more poetry when it became available, but had never been successful in finding a classic poetry book club.

Once we had completed the frames, my father would slide the pictures in from behind and secure them with metal posts. Then I would help him tap in two nails at the backs, and around these we would twine the string the pictures would hang from. We lived in a big house then, and there was lots of wall space for the pictures, and it became kind of a game, finding the places to hang them. We discovered an expanse of room on the stairway and hung an ascendance of pictures. I recall there were a lot of Goya portraits there, some Hals in the halls, a miscellany of Vermeer, Renoir, and Rembrandt in the living room, dining room, and den, Gainsborough and Lawrence in my parents' room, Degas in my room, and Caravaggio and Reynolds in my brothers' rooms.

I didn't know the titles of any of these paintings. For some reason, this information was not included on the backs of the prints, and I mused over many, trying to imagine who the characters might be, and (not understanding the concept of portrait commissions, which applied to most of these works) why the artist had selected these people to paint. I sometimes asked my father questions, especially if I couldn't reason satisfactory explanations for myself. A case in point was one of Goya's—a child in a crimson suit. I would later discover this work was called *Don Manuel Osorio Manrique de Zuniga* after its subject, who was a three-year-old boy. But at the time, I couldn't make up my mind if the subject was a girl or a boy or a child at all. There was something old and clownish about this figure who wore a golden sash and overly large slippers, something circus-like in the menagerie of animals—his cage of finches and his magpie on a leash. His audience of three hungry cats left me feeling even uneasier. Had this quasi-adult-child any notion that his cats were likely to eat his birds? My father went into a long-winded explanation, peppered with strings of polysyllabic words. In fact, he knew nothing about the painting, but felt it important that when we spoke about any form of art, we did so with great pretension and confidence. He said something about Goya trying to achieve the illusion of youthful aging in the picture, that the character was of course a middle-aged woman, and that her birds and red suit symbolized her conflicting instinctual and intellectual desires, while the cats, representing the three fates, were cleverly employed by Goya to demonstrate the character's dread of the future. I knew it was all bull, but somehow it made me feel a bit easier at the time.

The more prints we framed and hung, the more I found myself disturbed by what I saw. Was Rembrandt's man in the golden helmet crying or laughing? I shut my eyes. I tried a joke. "What do you get when you cross a millipede with a parrot?" I imagined the man listening. "A walkie-talkie!" I shouted and quickly looked. The man seemed to be sobbing. I closed my eyes again. "I hate to be the one to have to tell you this," I said very solemnly, "but your wife is dead." When I opened my eyes, I was certain the man was stifling a chuckle. When I talked to my father about it, he gave me a mini-lecture on ambiguity and paradox. He made me repeat the words a couple of times and encouraged me to add them to my list of three-syllable-plus words, "For future reference."

"You don't know if the man's laughing or crying either," I said.

"The artist doesn't wish for us to know," my father said confidently.

But the more questions I asked, the more my father's confidence wavered, until finally, he was forced to buy an art book. It was a large, thick book with a golden binding entitled *Treasury of Masterpieces*, and he brought it home shortly after I expressed my misgivings about Vermeer's *The Lacemaker*, a picture that completely terrified me. I was convinced that the figure in the painting was a Raggedy Ann-type doll. She had once been a woman, but some evil puppet master had transformed her and set her to this arduous task, forcing her to work day and night without rest. I wasn't completely certain what the task was, but considering the painful hunch of her shoulders and the alarming tension in her hands, I imagined it must be something quite impossible, like the task of spinning straw into gold which the king had set for the miller's daughter in my favourite fairy tale, *Rumpelstilskin*.

My father didn't think my reading of the picture was correct, although it was clear he couldn't form any kind of definitive thoughts on it himself. He granted that she did, in fact, look like a large ugly doll, and that indeed she seemed to be incredibly uncomfortable, but he'd commit himself to no more than that.

I found it difficult to look at the picture after a time, and if I had to walk alone through the room where it hung, I would always break into a run. I believed if I looked at it too intently, I would be transformed into a hideous doll myself.

My father spent hours pouring over the art book he'd bought, and when we next discussed the frightful picture, he told me, "Vermeer was attempting to express feminine industry as honourable." This was something I found hard to believe. Even though I didn't think it would change my feelings about the picture, I still wanted to read what the book said for myself. I challenged my father to show me the book, but he claimed he'd misplaced it, which made me even more suspicious.

I imagined that my father had discovered in his readings that the painting was actually cursed, that any girl who looked upon it would be transformed into a hideous doll on her sixteenth birthday and forced to make lace for the rest of her life. I was only seven, so I had a good nine years left and believed my father had intentionally hidden the book so my remaining human time would not be plagued with dread and worry.

Weekends passed, and while I remained frightened by *The Lacemaker,* I forgot all about the book. My father and I framed more and more pictures, and I started to become frivolous in my placement of them. I thought it was funny to put the Mona Lisa with her enigmatic smile directly across from the toilet in the powder room. I tacked the print of Millet's *The Gleaners* on a low hook, over the dog's dish, so it looked like the three women were picking chaffs of wheat out of his kibbles. My mother, who thought the pictures were tacky but couldn't stop my father from buying them, told me if I was going to be silly, she'd find me some real work to do, and I knew that meant rolling my father's and brothers' socks, so I promised I'd be serious and escaped to the living room where I could contemplate the divestment of the remaining pictures with as much impudence as I wished.

I'm not sure exactly what it was that made me look under the frilly-bottomed chesterfield; perhaps I was thinking, as a joke, I might put one of the prints there, but to my surprise, I discovered my father's *Treasury of Masterpieces* pushed into the far centre, flush to the wall. I knew that no act of absent-mindedness was responsible. My father had consciously hidden the book. Its placement was far too precise for it to be accidental, and with renewed fears over the curse of *The Lacemaker*, I prepared myself for the worst and determined to fish the book out. My arms were too short to reach it, and the chesterfield was too heavy for me to move away from the wall; so I turned my body around, sliding my lower half completely under the couch, then using my legs and feet, manipulated the book forward. I trembled as I opened it, fearing what I might discover. The books pages were glossy and exuded an unpleasant acrid smell. Many of its illustrations were familiar, but it was the greater numbers that weren't that wrapped my attention, making me forget all about *The Lacemaker* by exposing me to new and greater horrors.

When I beheld John Singleton Copley's *Watson and the Shark*, I didn't initially notice the panic and hopelessness of the nine men aboard the too-small boat, or realize that they were attempting to rescue the terrifying naked figure in the water, whose long blond hair billowed toward the open-mouthed beast. I noticed only the naked character's crazed upside-down expression—which made me feel as if my world had been upturned—and the shark's small fixed eye and human-like lips that seemed the only living parts of its head. I felt for the first time the fullness of that word *paradox* which my father had given me. The revulsion I felt made me sick, but I couldn't stop looking. My eyes crawled over the page, craving every ugly detail as my mind asked its questions: Did things like this really happen? Was the naked figure a man or a woman? Why was he naked when everyone else was dressed? How did he come to be in the water? I felt embarrassed for him, and imagined how humiliated and scared he must be; I wondered which was ultimately worse, being eaten by a shark or being naked in public.

The book's text answered some of my questions. The painting was based on a real experience, and the naked figure in the water was male, but how he had come to be in the water and why he was naked were not explained. I imagined he was unaware he was naked—that he'd needed some swimming trunks and unluckily had met the same con men who'd fooled the emperor in *The Emperor's New Clothes*. Somehow imagining this made me feel a bit less troubled, and I was able to turn the page.

Before now, I had never seen a nude, never realized that the naked human form was of such interest to the artist nor that any person would willingly allow themselves to be rendered in such a state. Yet here, in my father's art book, there was an entire section devoted to nudes, and as if this, in itself, wasn't shocking enough, I discovered that some of these nudes had been painted by the very artists whose masterpieces hung on our walls.

I beheld with fascination and shame Goya's dark-haired, voluptuous *Nude Maja*, who in her clothed form hung in our foyer. She'd never been a subject of great interest to me. I'd wondered only if her tiny, pointed slippers prevented her from walking, and that's why she was lying on her bed. Now, however, with this unclad identical likeness to compare her to, there were many points of curiosity. Her face, for example, in the two pictures was different.

In the clothed version, it was rounder and paler, and looked to me as if Goya had not spent as much time on its detail as he had in the nude painting. While the pose of her body was identical in both pictures, its proportions also seemed dissimilar. Her breasts looked much larger naked, while her thighs, in contrast, appeared much less ample. But my eyes inevitably returned to her feet and my mind to the question: How was it possible that a woman with feet as large as that could squeeze into those tiny slippers? The text that accompanied the picture speculated on the model's identity and said how the *Nude Maja* had created such a moral uproar in Spanish society that Goya had felt compelled to do another painting of her clothed. The text mentioned that both paintings came to be owned by Manuel Godoy, a chief minister, who hung them in a hidden cabinet for his own private viewing pleasure. The text even mentioned that a Spanish postage stamp of the *Nude Maja* had been made in 1930, commemorating Goya, and that the US government had refused to allow letters carrying this stamp into the country because they deemed it obscene. But the question of the Maja's large feet and her diverse proportions—the question I felt most pressingly needed to be addressed—was not taken up in the text and I knew that I couldn't ask my father.

I compared the nude Maja's feet with the slipper-clad feet of Manet's nude Olympia. I could see Olympia's feet were smaller, though I doubted even she would have been able to wear the clothed Maja's golden shoes. But the importance fell completely away, as I turned the page and beheld Rubens's petrifying *Rape of the Daughters of Leucippus.*

The word *rape* was unfamiliar to me, but it seemed likely it was some form of the verb *rip*, and the two naked women in the picture bore this out, as there were strips of fabric beneath them, which I assumed the two men in the picture had torn from their backs. I felt disgraced for these women and angry that, for some reason, even though they appeared bigger than the men, they seemed convinced they couldn't get away. I wondered if it had been the men's strategy to rip off their clothing so they'd be paralyzed with humiliation and unable to fight back. I thought if I'd been one of those women, even if I was really embarrassed, I still would have bitten the men until they bled and tried to poke their eyes out with my fingers. I thought maybe the angel in the picture would bite the horse and save the women. It made me think of one time when my family was visiting my father's friend, and my older brother started calling me names and hitting me. I pushed him into a deep swimming pool, even though I knew he couldn't swim. My father had been drinking and he came after me and pulled my pants down in front of everyone and tried to slap my bare bum, but I bit his hand and got away, and ran to the car and locked myself in. He came with the keys then, and everyone crowded around the car, but I just held the locks down, every door he tried, until it started getting late and dark, and I made him promise he wouldn't shame or hit me or I wouldn't open the doors. I didn't like remembering that and shut the book quickly, not wanting to remember anything else.

I felt ill after I slid the *Treasury of Masterpieces* back under the couch and wished I'd never seen it, but I couldn't stop myself from furtively returning to the book again and again over the next few weeks. It became impossible for me to look at the Rubenses, Manets, and Goyas on our walls without seeing nakedness and feeling ashamed, and then gradually, almost as if in self-defence, all of the pictures turned tawdry, and I supported my mother in her protests against them, and eventually they all became invisible. My father asked me why I didn't want to help him frame and hang the pictures anymore, and I told him it had gotten boring and that my mother wanted me to help her roll socks. Gradually, even my father lost his enthusiasm for the pictures, the gas station finished its promotion and started selling steak knives, and I took the boxes of unframed masterpieces to school to give to my art teacher, who cut them all up into small square tiles, which our class used to construct pretty, colourful geometric mosaics.

EASTER

EASTER 1968, I WAKE IN THE EARLY HOURS of the morning, unable to breathe. My mother pulls me from my perspiration-soaked sheets and runs a scalding shower in the bathroom. The sounds I'm making are unnatural. Heavy waves of steam unfurl, blinding and gas-grey. "Croup" is what she calls it. It comes upon me several times a year and correlates with holidays, just before we travel to my grandmother's.

My mother tells my father that she's tired, that the journey's too long, that she just wants a quiet holiday at home. My father says that his mother expects him, he has to fix her sump pump, she wants to see the kids. He accuses my mother of disliking her, which is true, but which my mother denies. She accuses him of caring more for his mother than his wife, which is also true, and which he denies. They fight and don't mention the homemade wine my grandmother makes and how at holiday times my father imbibes even more liberally than usual. They don't mention the terrifying journeys back home with my father raging and the car weaving all over the highway, and my mother trying to appease him so we don't get into an accident.

I wheeze and bark in the foggy bathroom, as my mother triumphantly announces I'm too sick to travel. I sense her relief as a kind of lightness, and I know that she'll be particularly nice to me now. She'd resigned herself to going on this trip, to being miserable, but miraculously, she's been reprieved. She fills the vaporizer, props pillows, and tucks me into her bed. My father is shaving and suspicious of my "convenient" illness, but knows he can't argue with the thermometer that displays my temperature of 102.

My brother brings my purple Easter basket. There's a large chocolate egg nestled in a bed of green straw. I feel queasy when I look at it. "Take the boys," I hear my mother say. "No reason you need to stay at home."

My grandmother lives close to Lake Erie where I swim and have fun in the summer, but I know it wouldn't be fun to go there now. When my father and brothers finally leave, it's as if a rock lifts from my chest, my temperature drops, and I can finally breathe.

The terms *dysfunctional family* and *codependent personality* have not yet found their ways into common parlance. Even as history is shattering the myth that all middle-class, nuclear families are happy ones, these families are fighting to preserve the sunny denials of a decade earlier. The situation comedy *The Adventures of Ozzie and Harriet*, though cancelled by ABC two years ago, still reflects the domestic persona my parents wish to convey. Like most of the houses in our suburban neighbourhood, the house we live in is bright and silent. We don't "air dirty laundry." We don't "let the whole world see." We don't speak about the bad things that go on in our house because we have faith that if we ignore them long enough, they'll all go away.

The TV shows my family most enjoy this year—*The Beverly Hillbillies, Green Acres, Bewitched*—all depict abnormal social units that either try to pass as normal or simply fail to see how they deviate. I rush home from school to watch the gothic soap opera *Dark Shadows* and engage with its mystery as if I were searching for a personal revelation. Things are buried, people have secrets, exposure is dangerous, and blood is sucked. It is eerily familiar, but at the same time makes me think that what I live isn't really all that bad. My father could be a vampire instead of an alcoholic. I could be faced with a choice: to drive a stake through his heart or let him keep destroying people. I'm glad I don't have to make that choice, glad I don't have to entertain this notion.

I'm all by myself in my parents' bed and it feels vast to me, though it's only the conventional double size used by most married North Americans this decade. When my parents have not been fighting, I spend my nights squished between them in this bed. It feels smaller then, suffocating, as if I'm being buried alive, but I welcome it when faced with the alternative of being alone in the darkness. My mother often chides me for being afraid of the dark. She complains about backache and says that I kick her all night long, and as much as I feel guilty about causing her discomfort, I can't stop myself from going to her bed. I try to explain to her that it's not so much a fear of darkness that's responsible as the fear that everyone in the household is sleeping—that everyone is unconscious and vulnerable to natural or supernatural attack.

Today, my mother carries my pillows and blanket and sets me up on the couch with my colouring books and crayons. She gives me orange-flavoured Aspirins, calls me "love" and lets me choose what to watch on TV. I'm feeling well enough to eat my chocolate egg. I wonder if my brothers and father are still travelling, if they've stopped at some restaurant for breakfast on the way. I'm sure my father will be in his "call me Boris" persona, wherever they are. When my mother is absent, my father never drinks as much. He likes to pretend he's "one of the kids."

In the living room, my mother keeps the television on, even though neither of us is watching it. She moves from her sewing machine in the dining room to the living room chair where the light is good for threading needles and hand sewing. Right now, she's making a dress for my Skipper doll to match the special Easter dress she's made for me.

Every Easter she makes me a new one and buys me new shoes. Sometimes she'll buy me a hat and a pair of white gloves, as she's done this year. The dress is made of a silky white fabric sprinkled delicately with raised pink flowers. It's sleeveless and full-skirted, and she's made a crinoline slip for underneath. She's also made, from cherry-blossom-pink material, a quarter-sleeve top that I can wear over the dress on cold days. The top buttons up the back and is trimmed with seam binding—pink and white daisies. My family doesn't go to church, but I think if we did, this would be exactly the kind of dress to wear there. It reminds me of a dress Hayley Mills wore in *The Trouble with Angels*. If I'd gone to my grandmother's house today, I would have been able to wear it. But I know the crinoline would have been scratchy and the dress would have gotten wrinkled. I probably would have gotten car sick and thrown up, so these are just a few more reasons I'm still glad I didn't go.

The dress is hanging in my closet and I ask my mother if I can put it on. This seems to please her, even though she says, "I thought you were supposed to be sick."

She lets me put the dress on, and I twirl and twirl in it, watching the full skirt parachute. I put on the shoes and hat and gloves and pretend I'm Hayley Mills going to church. As I make believe, I'm aware that this dress, like so many my mother creates, is not like the dresses other girls in my third grade class wear. My teacher, Miss Click, has a Southern accent, and always comments on my "gorgeous" dresses. When I look down at the ground and blush she says, "You're such a nice, quiet, modest little girl," and I feel the heat in my face extend to the roots of my hair. I like my teacher very much, but I don't like her attention. I wish she'd ignore me, like everyone else does, and let me remain invisible.

Invisible is the way I'm feeling right now, as I spin and spin in front of my mother, and pretend I'm Hayley Mills, and kneel on the floor and clasp my hands in prayer. I feel as if my mother doesn't see me, and I'm glad about this, because if she did, I know she'd say what I was doing was silly.

"You're a nice, quiet, modest little girl," God says to Hayley. "Thank you, Lord," Hayley says.

I think, perhaps, God doesn't know that Hayley smoked in the boiler room at St. Francis Academy. As I twirl and spin in my Easter dress and feel so good and pious, I allow certain facts to peel away. Once a week I ride my bike out to a field with my friend, Phoebe, who lives next door. She's four years older than me and has a bra. We climb a tree together and then we smoke cigarettes she's stolen from her mother. "For shit's sake," she says, "don't be a baby. Can't you even light a match?"

She has a younger sister, Aurora, who's blond and skinny and wears blue kitty-corner glasses. She's only two years older than I am and was my best friend before she stopped coming out to play. She started doing all of Phoebe's chores as well as her own in exchange for Phoebe's bra. I looked through one of their windows once and saw the outline of it under her shirt when she was vacuuming. "What fun can that be?" I asked Phoebe.

"No fun," Phoebe said. "My sister's an asshole twerp. She even stuffs!"

"Stuffs?"

"For shit's sake, are you dense? It means she sticks toilet paper into the bra so she doesn't look flat—but she's flatter than a pancake. She's flatter than someone who's been run down by a steamroller. She's so flat her titties stick in instead of out."

I don't have regular chores to do. Sometimes my mother makes me roll my brothers' and father's socks, which I find boring and can't do very well. "Practice makes perfect," my mother always says, but even at eight years old, I find it sad that anyone should strive to become a perfect sock roller. The job I like best is ironing my father's white handkerchiefs on my mother's big mangle iron. There are always hundreds to do, damp and wrinkled, coiled in a pillowcase to keep them moist. I remove one, stretch it in my hands, place it on the iron's roller. My right knee presses the little lever that sets the machine in motion. The roller revolves. A hot steel plate descends. The scrap of wrinkled fabric re-emerges from its ride twice as large as it formerly was, and perfectly flat. Flatter than a pancake, flatter than someone who's been run down by a steamroller, even flatter than Aurora.

My mother warns me to be cautious. She tells me stories of mangle iron accidents—little girls who've burned their hands right off, others who've been dragged in by their hair and dresses. When I ask her to repeat these stories again and again, she gets annoyed. These stories are not intended for my enjoyment: they are intended to frighten me into a state of vigilance, but what she doesn't realize is that I'm always vigilant; I'm always anxious and conscious of the possibility of disaster.

Phoebe and Aurora have a litany of set chores to do each day. Their mother, Mrs. Richardson, is "a neat freak" who spends much of her time shopping for antiques and who will "give them shit" if the house isn't spotless when she returns home. They do things we never do at our house, like make Bundt cakes from scratch, and scrub the places you can't see on the bathroom floor with a toothbrush. The houses in our neighbourhood are well insulated. They were constructed with privacy and noise control in mind; still, sometimes, when I'm jumping rope in our driveway, I can hear through closed doors and windows shouting and smacking because the girls have left something undone.

I feel sorry for them and often think that their life is much worse than mine. I'm rarely slapped, and when I am, it's either because I've done something very bad and believe I deserve it or because my father is very drunk. I think I'm lucky that I don't have to make a Bundt cake from scratch. I'm aware that just the number of chores they have to do opens them to the greater possibility of making mistakes, of doing things wrong, of forgetting, and of bringing the wrath of their mother down upon them. As I twirl and twirl in my Easter dress, invisible and pretending, I think of all of this before I let it spin away. Things could be so much worse, I think. Our mothers and fathers could all be vampires. We could accidentally discover their coffins. Would Phoebe and Aurora run a stake through their mother's heart? I see the scene in my mind's eye. "Thwack!" I imagine that they would.

Eventually, as she finishes Skipper's dress, my mother becomes aware of me. "You're supposed to be sick," she says. "Go and get out of those glad rags."

It's as if she's emerged from a trance or as if I've suddenly become visible, and although I know that being a vampire wouldn't be fun, I wish I had a vampire's power so I could put her back into her slumber and continue to remain unseen.

After I change, I'm back on the couch, under my blanket. I colour in my *Bewitched* colouring book, a picture of a coffee pot magically pouring coffee into a mug. The sun is setting and the sky is flaming pink. My mother makes me Campbell's chicken noodle soup and brings it on a tray.

I think of my brothers at my grandmother's house. They will have long arrived by now. She will have kissed them, pinched their cheeks with her thumb and finger, and pushed their hair back from their foreheads so she could see their entire faces. She probably has already offered them chocolate-covered cherries and suckers and given them each a dollar to spend at the corner store. They're probably just sitting down to dinner: halupsi, nalesniki, perogies and borsht. I think about all these wonderful dishes my grandmother cooks, as I sip my chicken soup. Still, I would rather be here with my mother, who is treating me especially nicely.

She speaks to me in a higher voice than she usually does. "Would you like more soup, love?" I say yes, even though I don't really want more, but I fear if I reject her offer, she might not call me "love" again.

As the evening sets in, my mother makes popcorn. She doesn't usually make it, but tonight is special, because it's Easter, and because we're going to watch the movie *The Ten Commandments*.

I've never seen the movie before and I want to ask questions, even though I know my mother hates it when I do. I find the movie gripping, my heart races and my palms grow damp. In spite of myself, the questions bubble over: "Why are all those people moving those big stones? Is that poor old lady going to get crushed? How did she get stuck? Isn't it only her belt that's caught under the stone? Can't she just take her belt off? Is that what happens when you get caught in a mangle iron?"

My mother says I'm ruining the movie for her and threatens to slap my bottom. She lights a cigarette and tells me I have to go to bed. I promise I'll be quiet if she lets me stay up. I bite my hand hard to remind me not to talk. It's difficult because there's so much going on that I'm not clear about. I wonder if God's magic is equal to Samantha Stephens's and why God seems to be able to do some magical things but not others. I wonder about the Red Sea parting and if all the fish and sharks and whales die and if the shellfish just lie there exposed and if people crush them with their feet. I wonder why, if God is so magical, so many people have to be killed. Can't he just put them in a trance like a vampire does and make them behave the way he wants? I remember to bite my hand, though, so I don't say a thing.

It is April 1968 and I am conscious of the value of silence. Asking my questions, speaking my mind, becoming too visible will inevitably jeopardize my position. I am silent and my mother lets me remain on the couch. When she's ready for bed, she carries my pillows from the couch to her room. I'm happy and it's nice to be able to stretch out without my father in the bed. When my mother turns off her bedside lamp, however, I see a shadow on the wall. I know that vampires can become shadows. I'd like to nudge my mother, ask her to turn on the light, tell her what's lurking in her cozy room, but I know she'd be annoyed. I know that she'd tell me I was being silly. So I pull the bedcovers over my head, close my eyes, and pray. "Dear Lord, please don't let the vampire bite me. Please use your magic to send him away." I say it again and again like a mantra, though after watching *The Ten Commandments* I'm not entirely convinced that God will be able to help.

In the morning, when I wake, I check my throat in the mirror for puncture wounds—there are none, and my reflection is still present. The light of day clears away all my terrors, and the vampire who stalks me from the wall has vanished. My mother is cooking bacon and eggs and making tea. We sit and eat in our nice, bright kitchen nook ignoring the chair my father once threw in the air in a drunken rage. The back of the chair is skewed and several of the bright golden upholstery tacks are missing.

My mother tells me if I'm feeling okay, we'll go to a restaurant later. She doesn't drive a car and so far there are no bus routes in our area, and I wonder where the restaurant is and how far we'll have to walk to get there, but I'm excited.

Sometimes, my father takes my brothers and me out to McDonald's or Burger King. We play "I Spy" and "Simon Says" while we eat our hamburgers, but I know my mother would find these games boring and so I don't expect her to play them with me.

All morning I anticipate our outing, wondering what it will be like, and imagining where we will go, and all morning my mother is extremely nice. She lets me watch the TV programs I want and brings me Oreo cookies. When the time comes for us to go, she lets me wear my Easter things. "You look just like a little doll," she says, as I skip along beside her. The crinoline is scratchy, I'm cold, and my new shoes pinch my feet, but it's easy to escape my body and ignore the discomfort. I just pretend I'm Hayley Mills and everything's fine.

The sun is high in the sky and our street is slick and shining. I know if vampires really do exist, they'll all be sleeping. As Hayley, I piously bow my head toward the tidy houses as we pass, trying to catch sight of orderly families joyfully proceeding with their afternoons. It's windy, and I raise my face heavenward, expecting to see Sister Bertrille sailing through the sky.

Besides *The Trouble with Angels* and the sitcom *The Flying Nun,* my infatuation with non-conforming holy sisters has been nurtured by *The Sound of Music* and *The Singing Nun.* The plot line is similar in all of these productions: feisty, imaginative, gifted women who exhibit unconventional behaviour enter a religious order. The "gift" presents a problem, and the woman has to make a choice between serving God or being personally recognized for her special talents. She inevitably forsakes personal recognition, even if in the end she leaves the convent. Perhaps I am enamoured by these Hollywood nuns because I want to believe that girls can have unique gifts, even if they're not allowed to own them.

My mother and I walk a long, long way. I'm getting bored and it's becoming more difficult for me to ignore my discomfort. The wind is getting colder, and I have blisters on my heels. I know my mother doesn't like it when I complain. When we finally get to the restaurant, we're seated at the window. We order hamburgers and french fries, and small glasses of pop as dark as blood. As I dunk my fries in ketchup, I think of nuns and vampires, and the drafty ancient buildings where they live. I think of my father driving home from my grandmother's house, weaving all over the highway, and I wonder if he died in a car accident if he'd really be dead, or if he'd turn into a vampire and fly home.

Throughout our meal, my mother remains extra nice to me. When I accidentally drip ketchup on my dress, instead of smacking me, she wets her napkin in a glass of water and carefully wipes the stain away. When she's paying the bill, she buys me a stuffed animal, a small squirrel, displayed near the cash register. "A special Easter gift," she says, and I jump up and down with excitement, even though the blisters on my heels make it excruciating.

When my mother isn't looking, I carefully lift my heels, and crush the backs of the shoes down with my feet. It's much less painful to walk this way and I know it's a long journey home. Outside, it's still cold and windy and the sky is overcast. My mother says she has a question she wants to ask me, and she wants me to be truthful when I answer.

I pick the flesh at the base of my thumbnails and nod. A hundred potential questions rush through my head: "Did you change your underwear this morning? Did you remember to flush the toilet? Did you cut your apple with a sharp knife on the good table? Did you use the fabric scissors on paper?"— I fear answering any of them.

As I shuffle beside my mother, holding tight to my wide-brimmed Easter hat, I know something cataclysmic is about to happen. I observe the way the wind is blowing before my mother asks her lethal question. I weigh fifty-seven pounds, which I know is thirty-three pounds less than Sister Bertrille, so I reason that with the hat on, there's a chance, if I can just find a place of high enough elevation, I could take flight and get away.

But my mother, whose voice has become very serious, asks the question before I find a platform for escape. "If your father and I got a divorce, who would you want to live with?"

In my mind I see a wooden stake, poised above my father's chest. Thwack, and the words tumble out of my mouth before I can stop them: small broken bones, ashes, dust.

"I wouldn't want to live with anyone. I'd run away."

"I see," my mother says, her voice no longer serious, nor kind.

There is a growing distance between us as we proceed home. I can only take small hobbled steps in my crushed Easter shoes. My mother's pace doesn't slow as she marches on and on, impervious to the cold and wind, which lashes my flesh and causes my ears to throb. I've become invisible and watch her, well ahead of me, passing streetlights and stop signs, until she finally enters the precinct of our tranquil neighbourhood, walks down our tidy street, enters our bright and silent, impeccably constructed house, and closes the door.

THE TRUTH ABOUT FAIRIES

IT'S 1969 AND WE'RE SITTING ON the Richardsons' porch. Phoebe squirts homemade suntan lotion into her palms—baby oil and iodine—which she spreads over her naked arms and belly. She wears a two-piece bathing suit that makes her look like she has breasts and lies on sheets of aluminum foil. With a comb, she rakes peroxide and water through her hair. Because her mother's gone shopping, it's okay for me to be here; it's okay for Phoebe to be here, too. She's abandoned her chores for the morning and helped herself to all these things she insists her mother won't miss.

She tells me that my flesh is the colour of marshmallows, and because I have black hair, I look exactly like a ghoul. She hands me the baby oil, and I slather it on my arms and legs. "Don't you know that blonds have more fun?" she asks, so I put peroxide in my hair and lie next to her, wondering when the fun's going to start.

Last year a group called The New York Radical Women staged a protest outside the Atlantic City Convention Center, where the Miss America Beauty Pageant is held. It hanged an effigy of Bert Parks, crowned a sheep in a mock ceremony, and tossed items of feminine oppression, including laundry soap, false eyelashes, and girdles into a trash can. "All Women Are Beautiful" was one of the phrases scribbled on protester placards, but I don't yet consider myself a woman, and lying next to Phoebe, I'm only conscious of my physical shortcomings: my baby face, my skinny, gangly limbs.

Phoebe gets bored easily under the hot sun and suggests we steal some cigarettes from a silver case in her mother's bedroom. We each take one, then collect our bikes, and ride toward the fields and forests that grow beyond the boundaries of our subdivision. She rides ahead of me, and I expect her to turn the corner where the Birdsells live. Mrs. Birdsell is out in the front yard and she calls to Phoebe. She's my mother's friend and has two daughters, Katy and Donna. I especially dislike Donna, who paints her nails with Just Like Mom nail polish and reels out phrases like "Let's call the girls for coffee!" She's two years younger than me and last fall my mother made me walk her to school. Our mothers had sewn us identical ponchos and some of the teachers thought we were twins. Although I have a terror of praying mantises, I would rather a horde of them march over my tongue than be considered Donna's twin.

Phoebe's talking with Mrs. Birdsell when I finally catch up. Donna and Katy are splashing in an inflatable pool in the front yard. "Are you two mermaids?" Phoebe asks, smiling. She bends to the pool and sprinkles a little water at them. They squeal like piglets and giggle.

"We're humans," Donna says. "There's no such thing as mermaids."

"There might be," Phoebe says, splashing them again.

"Mermaids are pretend," Katy laughs, and both she and Donna splash water back.

"Would you like Phoebe to babysit Saturday?" Mrs. Birdsell asks. It is 1969, and babysitting is a prestigious occupation for teenaged girls. In a middle-class neighbourhood, such as ours, a babysitter can earn as much as seventy-five cents an hour.

Donna and Katy shriek with excitement as my heart plummets. Donna is closer to my age than Phoebe. Is it possible that one day Phoebe will be asked to babysit me?

I'm happy to leave the Birdsells' and ride out into the country where soybean fields and woodland surround us and decrepit farmhouses stand on sweeping acres of land. The subdivision of Hinsbrook, where we live, has not yet become part of the city of Darien, a Chicago suburb. There are still vast spaces to explore, places not devoured by postwar progress.

Phoebe finds a thick-branched tree with crumbly bark that we climb. When we're camouflaged by leaves, she produces a cigarette and a packet of matches. "Donna and Katy are cute kids," she considers, "but they don't have much imagination." She lights the cigarette and inhales, then hands it to me. "Imagination is really important when you're little. It helps you cope," she says.

I puff on the cigarette and wonder what the word *cope* means. It sounds like it should be a cross between a coat and a cape, but that wouldn't make sense. It rhymes with *hope*, I reason, so probably has something to do with that.

When we've finished two cigarettes, we mount our bikes and fly over the melting black streets, back toward our neighbourhood. As Phoebe rounds the corner at the Birdsells', she suddenly picks up speed. I don't realize immediately the cause of her panic, but as I ride closer to home, I see what she must have seen—her mother's VW is parked in their driveway.

Even though the landmark book *The Battered Child* was published last year, the phrase *child abuse* is unknown to us. As the term becomes more widespread and used by our morally impeccable neighbours, it will never be applied to children in our subdivision, whose fathers are white-collar workers and whose mothers have the leisure to spend their days shopping and beautifying their homes. Only children who come from lower socio-economic backgrounds or find themselves in single-parent households will be "at risk." In neighbourhoods like ours, caregivers do not abuse children because they are well adjusted and normal and have no psychological problems. They do not exhibit "deviant behaviour" of any kind, for if they did, how would it be possible for them to live in such fine and tidy places, with mowed lawns and gas lanterns at the end of their drives? When children are slapped and beaten in our neighbourhood, it is called "discipline" and is as different from "abuse" as chalk from cheese.

By the time I pass Phoebe's house, she's already indoors and crying. I can hear Mrs. Richardson shouting and swearing and the crisp, stinging repeat of the leather belt she uses for whipping. I stand in the driveway listening and wondering. Will Phoebe call for help? Will she beg her mother to stop? I wonder if there's anything I can do to give Phoebe time to get away—ring the doorbell and run, make a prank phone call? But I know she wouldn't even try to escape. Any attempts to run would just be met with greater punishment.

Several days pass before Mrs. Richardson goes out again, and Phoebe appears on the porch, searching through old *Seventeen* magazines. She bypasses the well-read articles, "Fabulous Fashions and Beauty Gear," "Charisma, who has it?" "How to talk to a boy," and turns instead to the advertisements.

Hair is an anti-war musical that opened on Broadway last year. It is also something that men are wearing long and that hippies are still not washing, but to readers of *Seventeen*, hair is prominently a symbol of the feminine self and a mainstay of the numerous advertisements which Phoebe considers intently. Since 1936 a Breck Shampoo marketing campaign has featured full-page photographs of wholesome women with sleek and gleaming manes. This year, the young and rising models Cybill Shepherd and Cheryl Tiegs will be among the golden glossy sorority who sell this popular shampoo. Phoebe will select our prototypic fairies from such advertisements. One will be fair, like Katy; the other dark, like Donna.

I offer "Daisy" as a fairy name.

"For shit's sake, that's a cow's name," Phoebe says.

"Daffodil," I try again.

Phoebe rolls her eyes. "It's got to be something magical sound-ing…magical… but also it's got to have something to do with nature."

"Why?" I ask.

"Because, dimwit, fairies are supposed to be nature spirits. Don't you know anything?"

Eventually she comes up with "Moon Glow" (for the fair one) and "Lacey Frost" (for the dark one)—both names I enthusiastically approve. Next, she cuts a piece of blank paper into four squares and begins composing a fairy letter in small, neat print, using a pen that writes with hot pink ink.

Dear Donna and Katy, she writes.

We are fairies who live in your garden and we watch you playing outside every day. We would like to be your friends. Would you like to be ours? We are including with this note some special magical fairy cookies that we baked. They're very small, but they taste good. We hope you like them.

She signs the note *Fairies Moon Glow and Lacey Frost.* Then, we go into her kitchen and make two dozen tiny sugar cookies, each no larger than a nickel. We sprinkle the tops with coloured sugar that sparkles like glitter, then quickly tidy up. Phoebe says she'll attach the note and the little bags of cookies onto a tree branch in the Birdsells' yard when she's babysitting.

"What if they don't find them?" I ask.

"They will," she promises.

Fifty-two years ago, Elsie Wright and Frances Griffiths, two girls roughly the ages of Phoebe and myself, photographed fairies cavorting in an English meadow. For years they maintained the fairies' veracity, and a host of prominent adults, including Sir Arthur Conan Doyle, marvelled at the capture of this mystery.

The following day, Donna and Katy will marvel at the mystery of fairies, too. They will find the gift swinging from a young maple branch and run to Phoebe, thoroughly amazed.

"Let me see," Phoebe says, feigning disbelief when Donna shows her the gift. "It must be a hoax." She reads the letter and opens one of the bags of tiny cookies. "My goodness! These cookies are so small, it would be almost impossible for a human to have baked them." She pops one into her mouth. "Mmmmm...tastes magical," she says.

Any nascent skepticism Donna and Katy may have had vanishes. They gobble the cookies up and ask Phoebe how they ought to respond.

Phoebe helps the girls compose their letter to the fairies and tells them where to place it in the garden. They write:

Dear Moon Glow and Lacey Frost,

Thank you for the delicious cookies. We would like to be your friends. What do you look like? What does your house look like? Do you go to school?

Mrs. and Mr. Birdsell return home, and the girls can barely contain their excitement.

"Fairies, huh?" their father says, winking at Phoebe.

Mrs. Birdsell giggles dismissively. "Well, I know two little fairies who ought to be in bed."

When we leave the Birdsells', Phoebe says, "Isn't it great? Did you see how excited their little faces were?" She collects their response from the maple branch, and both of us are enthusiastic about the prospects of replying.

The next morning, before anyone on our street is awake, Phoebe sneaks over to our house and wakes me by throwing tiny stones at my bedroom window. I get dressed quickly and rush outside to meet her.

She's always been a good artist, and she wants to show me a few of the tiny, colourful pictures she's sketched, willowy winged fairy bodies in glittering shimmering dresses, whose faces are the exact replicas of the Breck Girl models. We sit under the stairs of her porch and quickly compose our next letter:

Dear Donna and Katy,

We're glad you liked the cookies and that you want to be our friends. We live deep in the bell of a blue flower—but please don't come looking for us. We get so nervous around humans that we have to turn invisible. We go to a special fairy school and learn things like how to fly and how to make different kinds of fairy dust. This year we're learning all about magic wands. We don't get breaks from school in the summer, because school is fun, and we don't need them. We're including pictures of ourselves with this letter. Always remember that everything a fairy gives you is lucky and will help make your wishes come true.

Once we sign the fairies' names, we race down to the Birdsells' house. Phoebe hastily ties the note and pictures to the tree and then we hide. Minutes later, we hear Donna and Katy squealing and shrieking and calling for their mother. Donna reads the letter aloud to Katy. "Come in now, girls," Mrs. Birdsell orders. "You need to get ready for church."

"But we want to play in the garden by Moon Glow and Lacey Frost," Donna wails.

"Don't you backchat me," Mrs Birdsell shouts. "You come in this instant or you'll get such a spanking you won't be able to sit down for a week."

When Phoebe and I hear the creak and slam of the Birdsells' screen door, we race back up the street. Phoebe disappears through her garage and I go back home to bed.

Over the following weeks, fairies Moon Glow and Lacey Frost make day and evening visits to the "fairy tree," as we begin to call it, delivering letters on scented coloured paper, and homemade gifts of fudge, peanut brittle, toffee, and bright little balls of modelling clay. In return, we collect Donna's and Katy's letters, full of questions about fairy life: *What kind of foods do you eat for dinner? What kind of material do you make your shiny dresses from? Are fairy wings see-through? Do fairies like insects?*

We had fun replying to the letters, fun secretly making the little fairy treats in Phoebe's kitchen when Mrs. Richardson is away, and fun sneaking around the Birdsells' house, dropping off and picking up Moon Glow's and Lacey Frost's correspondence.

Why is it that Donna and Katy believe in these fairies? What evidence of their existence, save a few small and carefully prepared treats and letters, do they actually have? In the years to come, Elsie Wright will confess that the photographs of the fairies were a hoax she and Frances Griffiths perpetrated, and in a televised interview will speak about the nature of human gullibility. "People believe," she will say, "because they wish to."

One day, Phoebe and I are confronted with a request. Donna and Katy ask for fairy dust that will make them invisible. We ignore it and offer more treats, but Donna and Katy won't be put off. *Real fairy dust that would make us invisible would be proof that you really are magical fairies. Our mom says fairies are only make-believe,* Donna writes.

These comments and our obvious inability to deliver such dust don't faze Phoebe. She combines epsom salts and silver glitter in the bottom of an envelope. *"Dear Donna and Katy, It's sad, but when people grow up they often forget that fairies are real. We're sending you the magic dust you asked for. It might not work on humans the same way it does on us, so don't be upset if you don't disappear."*

"Do you think they'll accept that?" she asks.

"They might," I say, more to humour her than because I really believed they will. I'd never have accepted it and silently congratulate myself on the maturity of my judgment.

As it happens, Mrs. Richardson is raging, and we're unable to get this letter to the fairy tree until the afternoon. Mrs. Birdsell has gone out, leaving her mother-in-law, who's visiting from Wisconsin, in charge. She and the girls are in the front yard, and it's impossible for us to hide from them. The girls are hovering around the tree and when they see us, run to us, sobbing. "Our fairies didn't come last night!" Donna cries. "Do you think they don't want to be our friends anymore?"

Phoebe crouches on the lawn as Donna tells her how the fairies had been regular visitors, how they had always left a letter in the morning, but today there was none.

"Maybe you've just been too close to the tree," Phoebe offers. "Maybe you should go into your house for a half hour and then check again."

"But they always come by morning!" Donna insists.

"Well, maybe they couldn't come as early as usual—maybe they were up late at a party or something."

Phoebe gently nudges Donna and Katy toward the house.

Their grandmother is standing on the front porch. "Fairies can be whimsical from all I've ever heard about them," she says, smiling.

"What's whimsical?" Katy asked.

"That means you can't set your watch by them," Phoebe says.

"I don't have a watch," Katy responds.

Donna and Katy's grandmother invites us in for iced tea. "It's a scorcher and we may as well have something cool and refreshing while we're waiting for those tardy fairies." She winks at Phoebe, just as Mr. Birdsell had done.

"You might want to go and freshen up in the powder room by the BACK DOOR," she says a little too conspicuously, but Donna and Katy don't seem to notice.

"Right," Phoebe says, "I'm so hot, I need to splash some water on my face," she smiles at the grandmother.

Phoebe is carrying the letter in the pocket of her shorts. As I hear the creak and click of the back door, I ask Donna to show me her new tea set, and encourage Katy to gather all her plastic farm animals together.

"Has it been half an hour yet?" Donna asks after only ten minutes.

I'm relieved when I hear the back door open and the grandmother calling us to the kitchen for tea.

"I want to go see if Moon Glow and Lacey Frost have come yet," Donna says. She and Katy slip away so quickly that even if I'd had to, I wouldn't have been able to stop them.

"There's a letter! There's a letter," Donna cries, running into the house again, kissing the envelope. Katy shouts for her to open it. Both Phoebe and the grandmother come into the living room carrying glasses of iced tea.

"Well, for goodness' sake," the grandmother says to Donna, "aren't you going to open it?"

"That envelope looks a little heavy," Phoebe says. "You might want to open it carefully."

"Fairy dust!" Donna screams. "Moon Glow and Lacey Frost have sent us magical fairy dust! I knew they would. Mom said they wouldn't. She said there's no such thing, but I knew they would!"

She tears the small envelope gently and removes the letter. A thimble full of sparkling dust falls to the floor.

"I don't know if I'd be playing with fairy dust if I were you," the grandmother says. "What if it turns you invisible and you can't turn back?"

Donna and Katy sprinkled the remaining fairy dust from the envelope over their heads.

"Oh, goodness!" the grandmother cries out. "Where have my grand-daughters gone?"

"I guess the magic dust does work on humans," Phoebe says, as if she's truly astonished.

"We're right here!" Donna says, grabbing Katy's hand. "I can see Katy. She's not invisible."

The grandmother looks vaguely in the direction of Donna, "Well, we can't see you, and that's a fact!"

Donna beams from ear to ear. "It works!" she sings. "It works!"

Both Phoebe and I know of the jealous fairy Tinkerbell, and how she appears as a light in the 1960 adapted, choreographed, and taped-for-television version of *Peter Pan*. We both know of her substance and personality, an illusion wrought by brightness and dimness and the sound of bells. She is more believable to us than Peter himself, who is played by a woman whose wires are detectable when she flies. The art of fairies, we have learned, is nothing but pretense and deception.

For the next half hour, the grandmother, Phoebe, and I make believe that Donna and Katy are invisible and try not to watch them as they run around the living room, lifting one object after another in order to shock us.

I try to act just as surprised as the grandmother and Phoebe, but I'm aware my performance is lacking because all I can keep thinking is how stupid and childish Donna and Katy are to believe that they're invisible—especially Donna.

Eventually the grandmother and Phoebe pretend that the girls are rematerializing. I'm happy about this because I'm bored and want to go have a smoke with Phoebe. Mrs. Birdsell arrives home shortly after the fairy dust wears off. Donna and Katy enthusiastically relate all that has happened. The grandmother nods her head in confirmation. I watch Mrs. Birdsell's cheery face rigidify into a smiling mask. "Is that so?" she asks in singsong.

When Phoebe and I finally get free, we grab our bikes and race out to the trees. We smoke our cigarettes in the top of a very sturdy sycamore, and then rush back to Phoebe's house to make fairy cupcakes, using a toy muffin tin, before Mrs. Richardson returns.

Early Sunday morning, Phoebe and I hurry to the fairy tree with a letter and some magical jewellery that we've fashioned from shimmering silver sequins and tiny pink and blue beads. We tie the letter to the branch and drape the jewellery over it, then hide beside the house so we can hear the peals of joy as Donna and Katy claim their treasures. But there's something different with the sounds of today, something heavy and discordant.

"I told you, NO!" Mrs. Birdsell shouts.

"I want my letter!" Donna whines.

"Get back into this house."

"No," Donna shouts, "I don't have to do anything you say. Moon Glow and Lacey Frost will protect me. I hate you. You're mean."

Then we hear silence, louder than the sound of coloured paper tearing, louder than tiny beads scattering on concrete. The life of a fairy depends on belief, and this silence is even louder than that.

Mrs. Birdsell hits Donna, and Donna screams. She cries for Moon Glow and Lacey Frost, begs them to come and save her, to take her away from this woman, her mother, whom she's never dared defy before.

But not a blade of grass quivers, not a single petal on a single flower budges in her defence. "There are no such things as fairies," Mrs. Birdsell shouts. "And no fairy is going to save you!" She drags Donna into the house by her hair.

Phoebe and I retreat amid the sounds of Donna's beating. There is no letter retrieved that evening or the next, no sign of Donna or Katy in the mornings playing by the fairy tree. *Dear Donna and Katy,* Phoebe writes. *We haven't heard from you in two days. We hope you're all right. Did you get our last letter and the fairy jewellery we left for you?* But there's no reply to this letter either. In fact, for two days the letter remains untouched on the tree. And then, on the third, as we tan on Phoebe's porch, Mrs. Birdsell removes the letter and gives it to Donna to return to us.

She is weeping when she approaches, and Phoebe goes to comfort her. "I know that you made up the fairies for us," she sobs, handing Phoebe the unopened letter. "I know you did it to be kind, but there are no such things as fairies."

"Who says?" Phoebe asks.

"My mother," Donna answers.

"Your mother's a grown-up!" Phoebe tells her. "Don't you remember—when people grow up, they forget."

"She showed me in the dictionary," Donna sobs. "It said fairies are imaginary, which means they're not real."

"Who wrote the dictionary?" Phoebe asks.

Donna hesitates, "A grown-up?"

Phoebe nods her head.

I remain on the porch as Phoebe wipes Donna's tears and convinces her to keep writing to the fairies. "You'll just have to do it in secret, and you can't ever let a grown-up know."

Donna sniffles and nods her head. She takes the envelope back from Phoebe and smiles. I feel all of the contempt I had for Donna disappear.

After Donna leaves, Phoebe and I get on our bikes and ride away from the concrete and the houses, the lawns and the fences, over undulating dirt hills through trampled grassy fields. We're excited when we find a mulberry tree in the middle of nowhere, its branches heavy with sweet dark fruit. We climb to its top, gathering all the berries we can eat, and smoke our cigarette with stained purple fingers.

"When do you think you'll tell Donna the truth?" I ask Phoebe.

"The truth?"

"About the fairies," I say. "That we made them up?"

"Never," she says.

I have visions of us as old as Donna and Katy's grandmother, visions of us even older, scribbling our fairy notes, making our fairy gifts, secretly delivering them to the fairy tree, day after day, week after week, year after year.

RED

RED IS THE COLOUR OF AGE TEN, driving from Chicago to Windsor, crossing the border at the bridge on Christmas Day 1970, rolling up the gravel drive of our new house. There are clay pits on either side that look like mass graves. On the car radio, Johnny Cash wails, *What is truth?* And the truth, here, is that there's no money, no work; my father can't stay sober and my mother's ready to walk. We three children can't shut up and can't stop wanting. Strawberry licorice, cherry suckers, the things we've touched that have left our hands sticky and red. There are wrappings tucked in the trunk, a red-handled toy pistol, a red-faced watch, and a doll's house made of metal, with red floors and furniture too small for any doll.

Johnny Cash is no longer strung out on drugs. He left his first wife and four daughters and was saved by God and the woman he married two years ago. He proposed marriage to her on stage in London, Ontario, a city less than two hours away. June Carter wore a blue dress and carried a bouquet of red roses. He wore a black suit and a red rose in his lapel. For most of his life, he played Martin guitars, but he bought a '58 Gibson J-200 before he hit the skids. It was red. He had his name engraved on its neck. It meant something to him. But it disappeared.

My father drinks beer from bottles with carmine red labels. The empties he calls "Dead Indians," and stores in the basement of our new house. It is 1970, and we have not yet begun to question the derogatory label *redskins*, although Johnny Cash, one-quarter Cherokee, has already recorded his album *Bitter Tears*.

Under this front porch, my brother will find a brittle arrowhead when searching for a ball, and we will discover that a native Indian burial ground exists beneath our neighbourhood. At the front of our house, there will be a red-leafed plum tree that will spring from a stick my grandmother shoves into the ground, but right now there is nothing. The house is the size of our old garage. We are short a bedroom, two bathrooms, a dining room, a den. Things we had. Things we will never have again.

A Franklin electronic Bible keeps scripture at Johnny Cash's fingertips, and a Navajo dream catcher keeps nightmares away. When I sleep, I dream of my dead grandfather. "He rests," I am told, in a cemetery not far from here. I have bright red shoes with square silver heels and I dance on the graves at the cemetery. I dance because, even though it has been snowing, even though it is Christmas, it is a beautiful day. Because the sun is spilling nectar from the sky, because I know the dead are lonely, I dance the sun through the soles of my feet, turn it red through the ice, and try to make the ground a little warmer.

One summer, when I am older, I go to my grandmother's house of pale red brick. There are powder-blue shingles on the roof and a clunky cement stairway that leads to the front door. At the back of the house, a wooden sun porch, redwood stained, extends out like a limb. There are screen doors and windows, pictures of angels leading businessmen across turbulent streams and a lumpy double bed that my brothers and I often sleep in together, though today I wake alone.

Red is the colour of anger, the colour of rage, not the colour a bull sees when a matador flicks his cape, but the colour an audience sees when the bull is stabbed and the matador gored. Red is the colour of blood, the colour of war, the colour that both my father and I find blooming like scarlet oleander flowers in our throats, the poison dimming our vision, slowing our hearts.

I told him to go fuck himself and die. I came here so I wouldn't be murdered; beneath me I feel the vibration of Lake Erie's tide. I smell the dark oil cans from the woodshed, and the strong dew-bathed mint that infests the garden and chokes the shrubs.

My grandmother gives me two stacks of wooden quart containers to fill with red raspberries and redcurrants. She shows me the ladder in her garage and gives me a bushel basket to fill with cherries and red plums. Sweat runs like red ants over my neck, down my back. I pick the berries off the bushes. The colour red stains my fingers, seeps under my bitten nails, runs through my chest in invisible rivulets.

Johnny Cash releases the album *A Thing Called Love*, and his song "Give My Love to Rose" is played frequently on my transistor radio. I seed all the fruit I pick with pictures of a boy I adore. Each berry I fill with him. Plums swing like dizzy heads. My arm stretches across the city. I pluck him from his home and bring him here to me.

Afterwards, my grandmother samples everything I've picked. "So sweet!" she says in English, and something in another language I don't understand. We sit at a burnt-red picnic table under a maple tree. In the fall, the leaves of this tree turn the colour of rubies. She produces a deck of playing cards and lays each card out, face down, then turns them over, one by one.

There are two red cards, a jack of diamonds and a jack of hearts. "Two boys," she says, "one a friend." She turns another red card over, a king of hearts, and then the ten of clubs. "Older man. Sickness." She turns other cards over, clucks her tongue, shakes her head. "Everything changing for you." A gust of wind blows some of the cards onto the lawn. She tidies things up and sends me to the lake. I feel she sends me because I need to be cleansed. I walk across a field to the place where private property ends, where public access begins. My feet move over rusty stairs, pound over charcoal-pitted sand. Carp lie angled there, silent red mouths half opened, seaweed twining in their teeth.

The sun is setting and water rises to my shoulders. When the current catches me, I let my body pour into the fullness of the lake. The beach dwindles to a single stripe. Legs and shoulders descend, my bloodshot eyes open in the murky, sudden cold. I could keep drifting, out to Michigan, I think. I could drift out to the skyline, to the golden buildings that pump effluvium into this solid pool. To the tired red sun, sinking into oblivion. I could drift and drift, and keep drifting into this redness forever.

ASHES

MY MOTHER: FIVE FOOT TWO, two-hundred-and-eighty pounds. Buried in a mountain of flesh, dressed in a shabby patterned muumuu, pink-scalped, platinum-haired, miserable.

She is the terror of the neighbourhood. God help the "holy rollers" who roll to her door with pamphlets on the world's demise. Just a tap, and she will open, making the prospects of armageddon as appealing as a picnic. And to neighbours who neglect to kowtow as they shuffle past her porch, she is equally unkind. She once said "Wipe that smirk off your face before I knock it off" to a friend of mine who had smiled at her. This was in 1972, long before he knew he was gay, or my brother came out of the closet, or the two of them became friends, then lovers, then enemies. It was before she told me, "I blame you for your brother's homosexuality!" then had a heart attack that left her with angina and a prescription for small, white nitroglycerine tablets, which she held, one at time, under her tongue. It was before I started high school, before Roe versus Wade, which might seem irrelevant, but isn't, since my mother had never wanted to have children, and all four times she became pregnant hoped she would miscarry, but didn't.

In her bird of paradise muumuu, which originally was red, not pink, it is difficult to imagine there was ever any other her—difficult to contemplate the sweet black-haired newborn, the cherubic infant, the pixie-faced child. All of these entities, bound to their mother, who was married to a second husband ten years older than her first-born son; a mother, whose own mother beat her as well as her three other daughters and put them into service at age twelve, where they scrubbed and cooked in the nether reaches of large, elegant British homes, never seeing a farthing of their wages because it was all poured down their mother's throat. My mother in her persona as "storyteller" tells me all of this and more. She tells me how her mother's first husband was cannibalized on a merchant marine lifeboat, and my uncle, my mother's half brother, who was something of a ladies' man, married my aunt twice and divorced her twice, and married two other women, before finally deciding my aunt was the only woman who could put up with him.

My mother tells stories of playing Ludo with her half brother and being angry and throwing tantrums because he wouldn't let her cheat, even when she was so sick with pneumonia, and how later he gave her a porcelain-headed doll he had won at a fair, and she named it Ruby, after his girlfriend—a girl he would have married if it hadn't been for the fact he'd made her pregnant, and she'd got an abortion in another city, and changed her name, and told him she never wanted to see him again. And my mother, in one of her fits, had smashed the head of the doll irrevocably, which in some mysterious, inexplicable way seemed to cap the relationship's doom.

There was my mother with scarlet fever, as red as if she'd been boiled, lying on a scratchy settee. And the night, in 1940, three days before Christmas, when the sirens shrieked, and she couldn't be moved, and her mother lifted the blackout curtains, and she saw round silver balls with fins and glittering showers and fiery splinters cascading to the ground, and the experience was ethereal, and made her think of angels. Her mother, who was not a particularly religious woman, got down on her knees and prayed: "Our Father..." And then, the following night, there was the drone of the V-1, "the doodlebug," which became suddenly silent in mid-flight, and the rattle of the ack-ack guns, and my mother, delirious, with a vision of Christ who reached for her hand, and when she went to touch it held up his other hand, and she knew he would let her live, at least a little bit longer.

And when the bombing raid finally ended, the row of houses in the other streets behind had fallen like a line of dominoes, and the other buildings that remained were still on fire, and Auntie Angie's Pekinese puppy, who was afraid of the sirens and had sensed they were coming, had run and hid, and had ended up flattened under piles of debris. And my mother had said, when she told me this last bit of the story, "Let that be a lesson to you," and she meaningfully nodded, and it didn't matter that I had no idea why, because she was already onto the next one, about another aunt, whom she'd lived with for a short time in the country. The aunt took in evacuee city children, and a couple had sent their boy to her to keep him safe from the bombs. But he was a "little devil" and climbed through a window in a tool shed to retrieve a bow and arrow, and after he collected it and was climbing out, the window dropped on his neck and killed him. This was another lesson, not about the dangers of parcelling children out to strangers, not about the impossibility of escaping your fate—it was a lesson about what happens when you play with dangerous toys and are disobedient. "Disobedient, like Pandora," my mother said, "a little girl, about your age, who opened a box she was told to keep shut, and unleashed all the evils of the world."

I cannot imagine my mother ever in the incarnation of Pandora, for the only forbidden boxes that she ever opens contain shortbread cookies and chocolates, which afterwards she guiltily hides beneath her bed; yet stories of a former her, who existed before the war ended, depict a young woman who was frequently disobedient and no stranger to the evils of the world.

Although I have no photographs, I see the woman she was then in a handsome woollen suit—a stylish jacket, an A-line skirt—cut down, re-seamed, patched up. Once a scruffy cast-off of her brother's, this outfit has been feminized and made attractive by the magic of her art. She wields the needle deftly and has learned to embroider, knit, and crochet, though in these times of shortage there is scarcely any material to work with.

She dreams of creating with luxurious fabrics, with silks and nylons, but these are all being used for the war—for airmen's parachutes and soldiers' tents and the rope that sailors use. Her passion for sewing grew in the shelters, for while the bombs fell, it helped her keep her hands busy. Others sang songs, some invented games, but she was able to transport herself to another time and space with the rhythmic transit of needle and thread. In daydreams she would imagine her own "House of Fashion." Even after her mother sent her to business college, and she learned shorthand and typing. And when she got her first job, working as a secretary for a barrister, the money she did not turn over to her mother went mostly to the unpatriotic and illegal purchase of fabric finery, which she transformed into full-skirted dance wear. This at a time when everything was rationed, when each person was allowed only four ounces of butter, twelve ounces of sugar, four ounces of ham, and two eggs a week. This at a time when even the most fashion-conscious girl was allowed only sixty-six coupons a year for all her clothing, and a half-decent frock needed eleven.

The government had control of raw materials and imposed "austerity regulations" on all attire. This meant that everything (pockets, hems, cuffs, and skirt widths) was restricted to a prescribed measure. My mother, in her incarnation of disobedient, didn't "give tuppence" for any government rules, but she paid dearly for the fabric, which she bought from a gypsy peddler, and cut—sinfully, on the bias—to produce a skirt that twirled; and if this were not bad enough, she took the skirt to work, packed neatly away in her carrier bag beside her gas mask and her dancing shoes, and when her boss left the office for the day, as he normally did, at one o'clock, instead of five (her usual quitting time), she donned her dance wear and off she went, like Cinderella going to the ball.

In the guise of Cinderella, she is another person, jitterbugging and jiving with handsome American soldiers. Her dark hair gleams under the dance hall lights, her red painted lips full and glistening. Her skirt twirls like a saucer. Her legs painted with make-up, eyebrow pencil seams drawn crooked up the backs. Her partner lifts her into the air. He flips her over his shoulder. As Cinderella, she discovers she is as weightless as ash.

At four o'clock, still wispy, she flutters back to the office. Her head is full of dancing, of the next dress she will make, of the squares of chocolate, cigarettes, and nylon stockings offered by the American soldiers. "Overpaid, oversexed, and over here!" the British troops say of them.

She unlocks the office door, steps inside, slips shoes from tired feet. She sighs and smiles—a smile of transition from princess to disobedient. A smile her employer sees before, as she puts it, "the game is up."

When she first tells me this story, I imagine her embarrassment. I imagine her tongue tied, rapidly becoming apologetic, attempting to convince him that some emergency had arisen, that her mother had dropped dead, or that she was a spy, called away for important war work. I imagine her pleading for forgiveness, begging to keep her job, fainting dead away. But she does none of these. While food and fabric are in short supply, there's an overabundance of jobs—a surplus of afternoon dances—a glut of handsome American soldiers. My mother puts her shoes back on her feet, collects her few things from the desk, and without saying a word waltzes through the door.

At this point in the story, I realize there will be no lesson—it is not intended for my instruction, but for the pleasure she experiences in recalling it. Triumphant youth is what she remembers, and the way it can shed wrongdoing like an iguana's skin and allow her next morning, without qualms or guilt, to find another job and move forward in her days, without thought of time's relentless baggage or the fear and misery of its increasing weight.

CEMETERIES

MY BROTHER RICHARD TAKES ME, perched on the handlebars of his bike, to Lake View Cemetery. Once, we used to explore the cemetery, pretending we were Hansel and Gretel, but now we pretend we're the different characters in Richard's first grade class: Peggy Bush, a squat, blond-haired troublemaker who pronounces *r* and *l* as if they were *w*; Mary Teresa Tarasa, a tall, obedient, dark-haired girl; Paul Burt, who is smart and studious; and Big Bob, who is always eating. The teacher, Mrs. Polorain, is strict and kind, and we begin our game with her leading the students on a class field trip past two statues of mourning women. They're cloaked and veiled in flowing robes. I pose as a statue next to them. Richard's classmates comment on my lifelike qualities. Peggy pokes me with a stick and I flinch. I try to recover my pose, but Mrs. Polorain isn't fooled. I'm forced to confess I'm an orphan. Mrs. Polorain dreads the thought of a child without an education. She sees it as her duty to adopt me as an honorary member of her class.

Richard and I play different characters—although we have our favourites. The only characters we agree not to play interchangeably are each other. We're influenced by Grimms's and Andersen's fairy tales and an array of cartoons and television programs. Certain movies not considered suitable for children, according to our mother, also influence our game.

At the site of the Collingwood Lake View Elementary School Memorial, where twenty-nine students who perished in the school's fire are buried, Mrs. Polorain notices a time machine. Before we have a chance to stand clear of it, Peggy presses the fateful switch that hurls us fifty-seven years into the past and into the raging flames of the school, where 172 children burned to death. As the fire alarm rings, Mrs. Polorain arranges us in single file and sends us down a stairwell to an exit. Peggy, who's at the front of the line, and trying not to do anything wrong, stubbornly insists we wait for the teacher to tell us we can leave the burning building. Mary and I try to push ahead and force the door open, but Peggy fights us to keep it closed. Meanwhile, Big Bob collapses from smoke inhalation and flames singe Paul Burt's hair. Richard arrives and says that Mrs. Polorain is dead.

My heart skips a beat.

"She succumbed to the flames," Richard says in a funereal voice.

"No, I didn't," I say promptly, moving into Mrs. Polorain's character, "and I'd appreciate you not telling people that I did, young man!" I wave a finger in his face.

"You're not Mrs. Polorain," he says bending his head toward the earth. "She's dead and may she rest in peace! She was a brave woman."

Richard and I are both aware of the advancing imaginary flames and know that we must resuscitate Big Bob, but I refuse to continue playing until he assures me that Mrs. Polorain is fine.

"If you quit now, everyone dies," he says, appealing to my guilt.

I walk right through the door we've created that Peggy is holding shut. "I quit!" I say, but then Mrs. Polorain arrives, her face blackened and her hair smoking. She resuscitates Big Bob and tells Peggy to open the door. It was a close call, she tells us, but she escaped from an upper floor just as it was collapsing.

Mary and I, both choking from the smoke, help Richard, Paul,

Big Bob, and the school children stay calm and file out in an orderly fashion. Once it stops smouldering, Paul sifts through the rubble and finds the time machine. We arrive back at the cemetery in the place the memorial once stood, but the location is without graves and eerily vacant.

"Strange, isn't it? Each man's life touches so many others." I know Richard is quoting the angel who saved George Bailey in *It's a Wonderful Life.*

Our family moves to Illinois the following year. We rent a house, and sixteen minutes away from our porch, the Forest Hill Cemetery, with its spear-tipped palings and dark arches, will become a new favourite haunt. It's right next door to the amusement park, Adventureland, where tall rides peak above the walls. A middle-aged woman attends an ice cream cart even in the dead of winter in front of a cemetery gate. "Buy a malted? Nice and creamy," she calls.

"No thanks," Richard and I mutter, shaking our heads, crossing the highway.

"Do you think that wady is cwazy?" I ask as Peggy, when we reach the other side of the road.

"Yes," Richard, as Mrs. Polorain, responds earnestly, "she never got over the death of her lost love, buried just inside those gates."

Although we've never been to Adventureland, it fascinates us. At home, Richard and I and his first grade class ride the tilt-a-whirl, the octopus, and the super italian bob, which is rumoured to be one of the three largest roller coasters in the world. We use the tree house in our backyard as a prop. Inevitably, as we reach the highest hill, Richard, as Peggy, drops a concealed plank of wood across the roller coaster's tracks, just to see what will happen. The plank derails the following cars, and hundreds of people plunge to their deaths.

"Oooops," Peggy says.

Fortunately, we've situated the cemetery in the park, so the dead are easily disposed of.

In late January, snow begins to fall. Kevin Stone, who lives across the street, climbs into our tree house with a BB gun and a hammer, and starts ripping it apart.

"Va goes ow wowwa coasta," Peggy laments.

I want our mother to call the police, but she won't. She tells Richard and me to come away from the window, where every now and again Kevin points the gun like he's going to shoot us. Eventually, our mother closes the curtains, shutting Kevin and his destructions out.

"Do you think Kevin is cwazy?" Peggy asks Mrs. Polorain.

"Yes, I certainly do!" Mrs. Polorain says, blinking. "And I intend to do something about it!"

Mrs. Polorain and I capture Kevin (played by one of my stuffed animals). We chain and manacle him with my mother's red headscarf and incarcerate him in a jail beneath the legs of the dining room table. We construct a courtroom like we've seen on *Perry Mason*. Mrs. Polorain presides as judge, I'm a lawyer, and the rest of the class is the jury. Kevin is found guilty and sentenced to the electric chair. Richard wants to be Kevin when the death switch is flipped. He wants to wear a brown paper bag over his head, as he believes all those who are executed must, and he wants to theatrically twitch on the ground, which he does for a long time after falling from the chair. Then he becomes Richard again, standing beside me, with that funereal moroseness. "It was a mistake," he says, pointing to the ground. "Peggy," he says. "She wanted to see what it was like to be on death row, and they took her instead of Kevin."

An anguished Mrs. Polorain removes the bag from the corpse's head, revealing Peggy's face, but before any more is said, I leap from the floor as Peggy and begin singing.

"You can't do that! Peggy's dead!" Richard says.

"Vat ewectwic chaiw was fun. Wet's do it again," Peggy sings. She flings open the curtains. Kevin and the tree house are gone, but the wind and snow have created drifts, and some have climbed up the back of the house. Richard and I bundle into our warmest clothes and take the class outdoors. Peggy finds and disturbs an avalanche, killing hundreds of people—innocent victims enjoying a ski outing on the "marge of Lake Lebarge."

"I onwee wanted to see what would happen," she says.

Richard and I both know the Robert Service poem *The Cremation of Sam McGee*. We decide to deal with the accident victims' bodies by burning them to ashes in an old boat, as the narrator of the poem does. Peggy accidentally falls into the crematorium when she's trying to stuff a body in.

"That girl is so much trouble," Richard says, as Mrs. Polorain. "I think we should just let her burn!"

"I agree," he seconds, in Mary's hoity voice.

"All in favour?" Mrs. Polorain appeals, lifting her hand.

"No!" I shout.

"Majority rules!" Mary counters.

"Majority doesn't rule!" I respond.

"You can't kill Peggy," I make Big Bob cry.

"That would be murder, and that's against the law," I make Paul say.

I go to the crematorium and remove Peggy myself. "Fank you," I make her mutter.

During this blizzard, ironically, our refrigerator breaks down and it's too snowy for a repairman to come and fix it. Our mother fashions an icebox outside, just beyond the patio doors. The following day when she goes to retrieve a bottle of milk, she slips and sprains her ankle, and I, after playing in the wet and cold all day, get sick and start throwing up.

"It never rains, but pours," Mrs. Polorain says sagely. She, Richard, and Mary read me Enid Blyton stories, scrupulously censoring every reference to food. Peggy, meanwhile, under her breath and in fake coughs, keeps mentioning it. "Cough, cough, coffee-cake; ah choo…ah cheese…ah chocowate baw."

I start to heave and tell Richard to quit it.

"What?" Richard asks. "I'm not doing anything."

"It's that troublesome girl you pulled out of the crematorium," Mrs. Polorain says. "Perhaps in future you'll know better."

"It smewed wike woast beef in vat whipped—cweam—atowium," Peggy says.

I throw up all over my bedspread.

We move to a new house in a better neighbourhood in the spring. The Clarendon Hills Cemetery is only ten minutes from our door. It's green and lush, and we especially like to walk past the baby graves, with their lambs and angels. "Into the arms of God" reads a stone's epitaph.

Big Bob and Paul Burt have all but vanished from our game and Richard makes infrequent appearances. He likes best to play Peggy and Mary and Mrs. Polorain, and prefers that I just respond to the characters he plays. He's turned both Mary and Mrs. Polorain into snobby, funny, outlandish characters, who both compete to be the most "mod."

"I bought my new mod hat on Carnaby Street, in London," Mrs. Polorain boasts, modelling the lampshade from our mother's new table lamp.

"I got mine there, too," Mary says, "but mine is better than yours, because I can make mine light up!"

"Am I mod?" Peggy asks, parading around with a shoebox on her head.

Mary and Mrs. Polorain laugh. "You're almost as unstylish as her!" Mrs. Polorain says pointing at me. "Look at that skirt! Did she buy it at Woolworths?"

We watched *The Monkees* on TV, and Richard had their first album. We played it on a portable record player we took into the garage. We also covered our father's workbench stool with blinking Christmas lights to create a go-go cage where I could dance. Then we invited all the neighbourhood kids into our discothèque.

After everyone left, Mrs. Polorain and Mary ridiculed me. "She was trying to be mod," Mrs. Polorain laughed.

"What do you expect for someone who hasn't even been to Carnaby Street?" Mary added.

I retaliated by ridiculing their stupid fashions, causing Mrs. Polorain to swoon.

"I'm afraid you've killed her," Mary explained. "She had a very weak heart. She didn't want you to know."

Because I can no longer take over characters, I goad her back to life. I make a tombstone out of cardboard. I write: *Mrs. Polorain/ Into the arms of God/She was stupid, and snotty/Had no fashion sense/And try as she might/Could never be mod.*

"What do you mean? Could never be mod?" she wails.

"You're supposed to be dead," I remind her.

I goad Peggy and Mary and Mrs. Polorain back to life so often that I want Richard to turn them into vampires like in the TV show *Dark Shadows*, but Richard isn't in favour.

"Fangs are definitely outré," Mrs. Polorain proclaims.

Richard has a hamster, Mr. Whiskers, which Mrs. Polorain wants to turn into a thoroughly mod rodent. She designs outlandish fashions for him from old socks and puts Vaseline on the top of his head to slick his fur back. Afterwards, Richard gives him a bath in a bowl of warm water and dish soap. The following day, Mr. Whiskers is near death. We fill a hot water bottle, cover it with a thick towel, and lay the shivering hamster on it.

"It may be an appropriate time to walk among the dead," Mrs. Polorain says in Richard's funereal voice.

It's late afternoon and the cemetery is desolate. We walk for a long time and see no cars, and then an off-white Valiant with big round headlights and a silver grill stops. The driver asks us what we think we're doing. He's blond with a crewcut and a square head. We tell him "Just walking," and he orders us into his car.

I grab Richard by the jacket. We run between headstones, far from the paths. Finally, we get beyond the front gates. "Do you fink vat man in the caw was cwazy?" Peggy asks.

"Yes, I do" Mrs. Polorain responds. "Who in his right mind would wear a crewcut?"

When we get home, Mr. Whiskers is dead and our mother is sewing at the dining room table. We tell her about the man. "I wish you wouldn't walk in cemeteries," she says.

She gets her wish a few years later when we move to Windsor. There are no cemeteries anywhere near our subdivision. All around there are new houses being constructed. Peggy, Mrs. Polorain, Mary, and I sometimes play our game in clay foundations of houses or out in the fields by the railroad tracks.

Over time, Mrs. Polorain grows more insulting and catty, Peggy becomes like Mary, and Mary vanishes from the game. In real life, Richard starts high school, and often I have to beg him to play. "All right, all right," he says when I badger, and I'm surprised one day when he initiates a class reunion.

Mrs. Polorain has written to Big Bob and Paul Burt, and Mary is flying in from England, where she emigrated to join the mod set. Richard and I and Peggy and Mrs. Polorain are going out by the train tracks to meet them.

"This is a very special day," Mrs. Polorain keeps saying. "I hope I'm dressed appropriately." Surprisingly, when I ask Richard what she's wearing, I'm told a plain dark suit.

"Where are your fashions?" I'm a bit disappointed.

"I wouldn't want the boys not to recognize me," she says.

"Do you wike my fashions?" Peggy asks. Richard tells me she's wearing a striking black dress and pillbox hat. "It's aw the wage in Pawis," she says.

It's summertime and the sedge is tall and spiky. Small brown grasshoppers fly into our faces and cling to our clothes.

"They're quite becoming on you, dear," Mrs. Polorain says to me. "After all, you need something to liven up that dreary outfit!"

We trudge on, closer to the train tracks, and in real life hear an approaching train's whistle.

"That must be them now," Mrs. Polorain says, licking her lips, rifling in her handbag for a mirror.

The train rumbles slowly past, and the engineer blows his whistle once again.

"There they are!" Mrs. Polorain exclaims. "Yoo-hoo!" She waves a paisley kerchief at the tracks.

I wanted so much for the boys to have changed—for Big Bob to have cast off his deprecating name and gained some self-esteem. I wanted Paul's genius to be recognized in the world. But both are exactly as they were—they haven't even aged.

Mary flounces off the train in a Union Jack dress, carrying a chic and expensive bag. "North America truly is the place fashion forgot," she says, surveying us.

"Did you have an accident with a flag, dear?" Mrs. Polorain asks.

After a volley of insults, Mrs. Polorain appeals for peace. "After all, it's a very special day today."

Peggy nods sombrely.

I don't understand at first. I just think we're all having a friendly class reunion, until Richard and Mrs. Polorain begin speaking in that mournful, funereal way.

"It's just about that time," Richard tells Mrs. Polorain.

"Thank you, Richard. You may never have dressed well, but you were always reliable."

"Thanks," Richard says.

"Come, children," Mrs. Polorain says, taking Peggy and Mary,

Paul and Big Bob, and leading them a few yards ahead of me, onto the tracks.

I shout to Richard. I ask him what's happening. I ask him to tell me what it is I should do.

"Just wait," Richard calls back. I don't like the solemnity of his voice.

He makes a train whistle in the distance.

"Stop," I tell him.

He makes the train whistle and chug and screech, as it tries to brake.

"Stop!" I shout.

"Come, children," Mrs. Polorain says, pulling them all close to her. "Goodbye, cruel world!" she shrieks.

In seconds, it's all over and there are five mangled bodies on the tracks.

"You can't do that!" I protest. "You can't kill them all off like that." I try to reanimate them, move into their bodies, goad them back to life, but Richard ignores me and begins walking home.

"Come back!" I shout. "They're not dead! The train didn't even touch them." I try to make Peggy sing.

Richard is growing smaller in the distance, his body diminishing with every step. It's as if he's shrinking, and when he's no larger than an ant, he vanishes behind a row of houses as I continue watching.

WISHES

THE MOON IS A SILK VEIL, tangled in the tree by the railroad tracks, and I make a wish for love on the first bright star I see, not realizing it's Venus. Soon other stars will fill the sky and cold, dark nights will freeze them in the lonely heavens, but it's summer now, and I send my wishes up to her.

My best friends have already become attached to boys—the clique that plays hockey and basketball in our neighbourhood and tells dirty jokes. These boys don't like me because they think I'm strange. "You're not like other girls," they say, and when I ask for clarification, they use my asking as an example. "Other girls wouldn't ask. They'd just go home!"

I tell them that I ask because I want to understand—because I wish that they would like me. They say they will never like me, because I use too many big words. I try to explain that I can't help it, that since I first began speaking, my father paid me a nickel for every three-syllable word I used, but they say the big words aren't the only reason. When they invite us girls to play football, I always take it seriously and act like we're really playing, when in fact they only include us because they want to touch our breasts. I don't think of these boys when I wish on the star, or any boy at all—it is rather a feeling I imagine—a feeling that, at fourteen, I'm too young to explore.

I have not yet had a real boyfriend, though I almost did. His name was Steven Styles and he was in my grade eight class. He'd failed a grade and was a year older than me, and he wasn't part of the neighbourhood clique. His family moved to Windsor from Michigan the summer before. Rumour had it he'd been in trouble with the police and was on some kind of probation. His parents rented a house in a good neighbourhood, and Steven asked the most popular girl in the school, Marilyn Holmes, to go out with him.

I hung around with Marilyn a lot then. It wasn't that we were really friends; I was just one of her coterie, and I liked to watch and smell Steven Styles. He had intense blue eyes and used Aramis deodorant, and because his parents and older sister had all found jobs in Windsor, his empty house became our refuge after school. This was the place where Steven and Marilyn made out, the place we listened to Led Zeppelin's *Houses of the Holy* cranked up so loud that the windows rattled and almost broke. This was the place where Bobbie Laplante fractured his arm in the middle of winter when he dove off the roof into the Styles's swimming pool, and the place Steven drenched the kitchen floor with butane and tossed a match on it, just to see what would happen. A fire truck came, but by then the butane had all burned away into melted linoleum and we'd been able to put out the long curtains that hung at the back door.

His parents didn't hit him when they came home, even though the police had called them, and they'd had to leave work. His mother looked nervous and his father looked burdened, but this was nothing unusual: they always looked this way. They didn't shout or send him off to military school, like most of the parents we knew would have done, but asked him if he understood why it was necessary he be punished. He said he did, and they negotiated his punishment. Steven agreed to be grounded for a week, which meant he had to come home directly after school. He always did this anyway, but his parents didn't know.

His house was the place I first saw and touched a condom. Steven bought some to experiment with, but ended up filling most of them with water and dropping them out of the bathroom window to see if they'd bounce or explode when they hit the ground. I don't know if his house was the place where Marilyn lost her virginity, or if she'd lost it before then. There were rumours she was on birth control pills, that her mother had arranged it because she didn't want Marilyn to be as ignorant about sex as she'd been when she'd married. Steven's house was the place where Marilyn first started smoking cigarettes. Steven smoked. His parents allowed it. They explained it would be hypocritical for them to insist Steven not do it while they did. They also believed telling Steven he couldn't smoke would only make him want to be dishonest and would work against "fostering an open dialogue."

Sometimes I came to Steven's house by myself at night when my father was drinking and my parents were fighting. I'd come to help him learn spelling test lists or study for math quizzes. He didn't want to study, he never did homework, but he was failing grade eight, and I thought I could help him pass. He'd put on Led Zeppelin when we studied, even when his parents and sister were home, and when the windows started rattling, his mother would knock on the door of the rec room, first almost inaudibly, then louder until he told her to come in. "Would you mind turning that down a bit, honey?" she'd shout. "Sure, Mom," he'd reply, but the volume on the record player never went that much lower, and the windows still rattled.

Steven's house was the place I came the night my father dumped our Great Pyrenees dog, Caesar, in a pumpkin field in Essex. I had not expected he'd really do it, and drove with him in his cold shroud of rage that dark night, trying to explain why I could no longer take the dog for walks. When female dogs were in heat in our neighbourhood,

Caesar became a maniac. At 110 pounds, he weighed more than me, and the last time I'd taken him out, he'd tried to break from the leash. When I'd yanked him back, he growled and lunged at my throat. He didn't bite me, but he knocked me down. Now he was breaking his chain in the backyard and jumping over our six-foot fence. Neighbours were complaining and threatening to take my father to court.

"All because you won't take the poor beast for a walk," my father uttered, not having heard a word I'd said.

It was raining lightly, and the black highway glistened. Caesar restlessly paced in the seat behind us as my father pulled over and brought the car to a stop.

"You can't just drop him off here, in the middle of nowhere," I protested.

My father opened the back door, patted the dog on his head, and set him free. He sniffed the ground, walked a few feet out into the field, and then bolted. My father believed it was possible that some farmer would adopt him—that he might end up with a happy life on a farm somewhere. "Poor dumb animal," my father said as he drove away. I was certain he'd turn and go back, certain he couldn't just leave the dog like that, but he did.

All the way home he told me what a useless, lazy girl I was, how irresponsible, undependable, and selfish. All the way home I'd tried to explain that I couldn't take the dog for walks; that I feared the dog. I tried to get him to see he was being unfair. Caesar had been bought for my older brother, anyway. Why did the job of taking him for walks fall to me?

My father told me to shut up, he told me he couldn't stand my back chat, he told me that he and my mother wished I'd never been born, and then he told me that he loved the dog that he'd just abandoned more than he'd ever loved me.

I ran to Steven's house that night, after taking a bottle of Aspirin and carving some letters into my arm with a razor blade. I ran to

Steven's because I wanted to die. Steven's sister called the suicide prevention hotline as I wouldn't let her take me to a hospital. Steven's mother made me drink water and told me to stick my finger down my throat so I'd vomit. Steven kept saying, "This is really a bad scene, Mad. You can't do things like this." His sister and mother were telling me that the best thing I could do was get some counselling; that counselling would be good for my entire family. I knew my family wasn't the type, and I was embarrassed because I wanted to die and now Steven's whole family knew it.

After I'd vomited a few times and the spacey feeling from the Aspirins left, Steven walked me home, because I said I had to go and I didn't want a ride. He walked me all the way to the bottom of my driveway in the pitch-black night in the drizzling rain.

"You're sure you'll be okay?" he asked.

I didn't know, but was glad he wanted me to be, and nodded and went inside. I crept past my mother, who'd fallen asleep on the couch in front of the television, as she often did. "The Star Spangled Banner" was playing the network's sign-off, and everyone else in the house was in bed. I recall the moon that night was full, a Cyclops eye, miserably staring through the window of my room. I recall the dreadful knot in my throat, and the crushing feeling of loneliness.

The following day, muddy and bewildered, Caesar found his way home. My father embraced him and wept, then dried his fur with my mother's good towels. He apologized to the dog as he stroked him and promised he would never abandon him again. I waited, hoping he might apologize to me, too.

My mother said he needed to get the dog neutered. She said it was the only way to stop him from jumping the fence and roaming, but my father said he would never neuter Caesar. It was cruel and unnatural, he said, to deprive any creature of its maleness.

At the end of spring, Steven said his family was going back to

Michigan in the summer. Some boys at the school said this was because Steven's US probation period had come to an end. Marilyn's and Steven's families had gone on a holiday together and talked about maintaining contact and spending time together, even after the move. "We're only going over the river," Mrs. Styles said to all of us who had virtually lived at her house. "You can all come and visit us, and Steven will come and visit you." But we knew it wouldn't happen.

There were days that followed when I couldn't drag myself from bed. My alarm clock sounded, but I didn't hear it. My mother tried to rouse me, but she said I swore at her and told her to leave me alone. My father was drinking even more than usual, and my parents' arguments were growing increasingly fierce. Frequently, I was at the centre of their arguments. "She's lazy, just like you!" my father would hurl at my mother. "She's nothing like me," my mother would shout back. "She's a bloody loser, like you!"

I was "less than useless," according to my mother, and "useless as tits on a board," according to my father. When school ended, my parents stopped arguing long enough to mutually agree to send me to my grandmother's house in Colchester. I didn't want to go at first. I knew Steven would be leaving at the end of summer, but there was so much tension in the house, so much anger, that in the end I was happy to go.

I was allowed to ask my girlfriend, Jes, to come. My parents liked her and thought her a good influence. I hadn't seen her for a long time. She'd started high school in the fall and didn't even know who Steven Styles was. She was very pragmatic about boys, and when I told her about him, she said, "He's going to move! He's not even available. Just erase him from your mind."

We woke at seven each morning and filled baskets full of berries. Then we manned the fruit stand at the front of my grandmother's yard. When it became very hot, my grandmother brought out her large sun umbrella and took over, allowing us to go to the beach.

The transparent moon tugged the waters of the lake. Our hot flesh steamed as we waded in. A greasy lifeguard, close to thirty, asked Jes if she'd go drinking with him. We both laughed, and avoided him. There was something surreal in the heat of the day, lying stretched out on my grandmother's towel, looking down the expanse of sand, my eyes only partially open, watching waves of heat rise, feeling my body become a meadow of sweat, feeling a tension within myself, a coiled spring, a snake, a noose.

I saw a diffusion of people, the camps they had made for themselves, the territories of towels and lawn chairs and inner tubes, the bottles of suntan oil and beach bags. The blue of the sky was strange and unearthly, like the shade of Steven's eyes, and the water, a mossy green, heaving to the shore, unfolding long white foaming fingers, and then I saw two familiar figures in the distance moving just beyond the water's reach. Blinding sun spilled into my eyes, and I told myself it was only the heat. In a desert, one thirsts for water and imagines an oasis; at an oasis, one must imagine something else. I imagined Steven, and the night he'd walked me home. "You're sure you'll be okay?" he'd asked. I heard his voice, just as if he'd said it.

"Go back to sleep," Jes said, hitting me with her sun hat. "It's not Steven. You're hallucinating." I wondered then, and for many days after, if I'd imagined him into being.

It was an odd coincidence, a strange synchronicity, the type no self-respecting author would allow in a plot for fear of being branded heavy-handed, but Bobbie Laplante also had a grandmother in Colchester, and he had been allowed to bring Steven for a two-week visit.

There were odd colours on the beach that day. The sand appeared a Sumerian red, the sun shone violet. I felt awkward and strangely self-conscious, aware of how my swimming suit exposed my flesh, aware of every sensation.

Steven told us that Marilyn had gone on a camping trip with a friend; that both he and she thought it best they start learning to spend more time apart.

Back at my grandmother's house, Jes said: "Tell him you have a thing for him." Did I have a thing for him? I wondered.

The colours and textures of the days remained surreal. The blood of the raspberries we plucked stained my flesh, and the chorus of nocturnal crickets echoed in my head. I lived and relived that night, driving with my father, seeing the tail of our trusting dog happily swish away in the darkness, the pills, the razor's blade, Steven's guileless face.

"If you don't say something to him soon," Jes said, one day on the beach, "I'm going to have to." I couldn't explain it to her, this constant rerun—Steven's voice in the drizzling darkness—and I was mad at her when she finally wrote, with jet-black charcoal on a flat white stone so he would see, "Mad loves Steven." I stood and walked away.

Seagulls, like white-feathered boomerangs, skimmed the muddy lake for food, and I thought I would walk on and on forever, beside them, until night fell, and the sliver of pale moon darkened, and stars invisible by day ignited the warm summer sky.

FETTERS

INSIDE THE NARROW AZURE BOX is a sterling silver bracelet: twin strands of chain woven together, connected by spirals to a rectangular bar. I don't see, at first, that the bar is engraved with my name—a looping and graceful cursive.

He explains that "the guys" are responsible. They said: "I don't see *your* name on her." He explains that the bracelet is a gift of possession. "If they try that again," he says, "I can just show them this. I can show them you belong to me."

He clasps the bracelet on my left arm. It's the nicest gift anyone's given me, the only gift I've ever received from a non-familial male. The fact that my name is on the bracelet, and not his—that no matter how much he shows his friends, they will not see his name—doesn't make his gift any less brilliant or his story any less sweet.

We make out in his father's car at Pillette Dock. I'm self-conscious of my breath and saliva. I wear pink peppermint lipstick, spray my tongue with Binaca whenever I get a chance, and try to choreograph our mouth-to-mouth contact so that strings of clinging spit need not embarrass us. He has a moustache that scratches my face. I try to ignore it. I try to move outside of my body, to escape the discomfort, to observe our kissing from a distance, where I can see myself as someone different, someone who's not so self-conscious or insecure.

The boy I'm kissing is three years older than me. He's also a foot taller. His age allows him to do things it's illegal for me to do, like drive a car and hold a part-time job. He's a senior at our high school while I'm a freshman, and I worry about him going off to university next year and leaving me behind. I imagine him dating university women, who are smart and pretty and sophisticated. I imagine him saying, "What did I ever see in you?" I don't know what he sees in me. Why he wants to kiss me. Why he wants me to belong to him. I know that I'm not the kind of girlfriend I'd pick if I were a boy like him. He's cool and self-possessed, like the rock stars in the posters on his bedroom wall. There's one of Keith Emerson, riding a motorcycle, that looks exactly like him.

When his parents are out at their lodge and his sister's at work, we lie together on his single bed in the darkness. We make out listening to Olivia Newton John singing "I Honestly Love You." He thinks she's a fox but wouldn't want the guys to know he'd bought this record. Female vocalists aren't where it's at.

When he moves his hand over my sweater and presses it hard against my breast, I pull away, embarrassed because my breasts are small. I've only been wearing a bra for a year, and the one I wear is blue and childish, made of cotton and elastic, without lace or padded cups or metal clasps, not like the bras I've seen other girls in my gym class wear. Still, I try and pretend we're lovers in a movie, but when his cold hand crawls under my sweater, I can't stop myself from pushing it away. When he drives me home, I want to apologize and explain, but know that this is impossible. To speak of shame is just as humiliating as those things that cause it.

The curtains of my house are open, and the yellowed sheers soften the picture of our living room. I'm always surprised at how warm and uncluttered it looks from the street: my father's watching a movie;

my mother's knitting a sweater. A stranger passing would suppose a cosy domestic scene and I wish to imagine this too, to linger outside, but I'm aware of the boy in the car, that proper dating etiquette requires he wait until I go in. If I hesitate too long, he's likely to find it strange, maybe wonder if there's something wrong with me.

I climb the concrete porch stairs, hold onto the window's warm picture as he drives away. I think of the old *Patty Duke Show*, imagine myself as the wholesome, teenaged Patty arriving home after a date.

"Look, Daddy! Look, Mummy! Look what he gave me!" I extend the bracelet. My voice is false and high. My father's skeletal face grimaces; my mother asks if she can get him something for the pain. "Nice," he exhales, not looking toward the bracelet, creases deepening in his face as he moves.

It should be obvious to me that my father's dying; that my mother's wrestling with guilt and grief. It should be obvious that my presence here threatens to disrupt the intense focus they need to navigate their private hells. When I look in the mirror, my father's eyes look back at me: linear accelerators with beams sharper than cobalt. I was born with his eyes, and hair, and have developed the gap he has in his teeth—a midline diastema—a lucky gap, some people call it.

I do not recall when his cancer was first detected or when his first surgery took place. I remember only that there had been a storm in April, and the sky had grown so black it was as if a god had turned and cast his shadow on the sun. My friends and I, immune to fear, danced amid the lightning bolts and flying trash cans. It was a game we played, a kind of dodgeball. A mile away, a concrete curling club collapsed; a tornado (the fifth deadliest in Canadian history) lifted and flung the club's roof into a parking lot.

My father, if he'd been home, would not have let me venture out into that storm. At some point he'd had surgery, then afterwards, radiation, which made him feel sick—and then, chemotherapy, which made him sicker. The incision in his lower abdomen refuses to heal. He stretches out on the living room couch in a swathe of loose-fitting clothing. Everything that touches his flesh causes him pain.

I know if he were well now, he wouldn't allow me to date this boy. It would be a traumatic ordeal with him dramatically forbidding me, standing on the porch steps and bruising my arm with his grasp, calling the boy's parents, following us in his car. It would be humiliating to me, and in the end, I wouldn't see the boy because I would feel so ashamed. But as it is, he does not indicate disapproval, and so I play-act that it's his inclinations rather than his illness that make it so.

In my room, I listen to an FM station on the radio and try to gather all the names of rock stars as they crackle past. The boy I date, "my boyfriend"—it's strange as well as thrilling to even think these words—knows all of their names. He buys *Circus* magazine, *Creem*, and sometimes *Rolling Stone*. He composes extensive genealogical trees of bands, showing the relationships between each group and where each member began his career. I'm terrified of making an unforgivable blunder, of referring to Donald Fagen as "Steely Dan" or Robert Plant as "Led Zeppelin." My boyfriend has contempt for those who do this. When I'm uncertain of a name, I say nothing.

There are a number of other things he dislikes that I'm careful of, too: gym shoes, midi skirts, red lipstick, ponytails, runs in nylon stockings. There are foods he disdains that I remember never to eat: vanilla ice cream, dark chocolate, margarine, milk. I make his likes my likes: hot dogs, baked beans, the colour black.

When I go to bed, I leave the radio on low and turn the lights off. The cold full moon stares through my window and makes my unruly thoughts unfurl. A few weeks after his chemotherapy, my father believed he was cured. My aunt, his sister, began visiting more frequently. She'd survived two bouts of cancer, and tried to convince him to see a doctor in the United States. She lives in Michigan, in a place called Livonia. "People Come First" is her city's slogan. She visits every week now in an inky blue Cadillac Deville. Each year, she gets the latest model, including this one, despite the Arab oil embargo that's jacked the price of oil up by eight dollars a barrel and has Nixon banning Sunday gas sales and begging homeowners to turn their thermostats down. Her husband is just under seven feet and "He needs the leg room," she explains. She's diminutive, two heads shorter than I am and built on an entirely smaller scale. She's tough and wiry, a straight shooter, who's known for both tactlessness and wisdom, and it rankles my father whenever she tells him directly that it doesn't look like he's getting any better.

My life has taken on a hazy quality, and the experience of living with the ravishing effects of my father's disease, its smell and appearance, its ugliness, has pushed me somewhere outside of myself. Every time I see him, he seems to have grown a little more skeletal and a little less human-looking. Bachman–Turner Overdrive's song "You Ain't Seen Nothing Yet" plays on the radio, and I wonder what it is I have yet to witness.

I try to turn the tide of my thoughts; try, instead, to think about the way it used to be, when I was little. I thought my father was a giant. He'd lift me on his shoulder on the sidewalk just outside of our house, and tell me to catch the moon, but I hear him cough in the living room, and it shatters this memory. It's best not to think of him at all.

My boyfriend is a stock boy at the IGA. He works there Tuesday and Wednesday after school, and today, Friday, the graveyard shift, from 10 p.m. to 6 a.m. He tells me stories about the things he does at work—how he and the guys mess around: spray whipped cream into *Penthouse* centrefolds, pretend they're masturbating the kielbasa in the deli, draw obscene pictures and list the phone numbers of slutty girls on the bathroom walls. The pockets of his jacket are crammed with little packages of Life Savers. "It's not really stealing," he says. "The boss expects us to take things."

His favourite Life Savers are cherry and lime, and sometimes when we kiss, we make a game of sharing one, of pushing a candy back and forth into each other's mouth with our tongues, until it becomes a thin fragile band. I have conflicting feelings about this game: it breaks the monotony of long make-out sessions, and Life Savers taste good. On the other hand, there's so much more saliva to deal with, so much more potential for humiliation. It requires a great deal of skill, dexterity, and concentration on my part to make the transfer effortless for both of us, to appear as if I'm always having fun.

Besides giving him an inexhaustible supply of Life Savers, my boyfriend's job allows him to buy records and magazines, to put gas in his father's car when we go out, and to offer to take me to dinner. I go to dinner once with him to his favourite Chinese restaurant, but I can't eat a thing. I worry that I might not use my knife and fork properly, that I'll drop food on my lap, that I'll take bites that are too large or too small, that my mouth will look funny. Before his illness, my father always monitored my table manners. If I didn't use my cutlery properly, he'd stand behind me and take my hands. "Eat the food, don't hurt it," he'd say, forcing my fingers down, making me cut everything up into tiny pieces.

My boyfriend fills his plate. "I'm not hungry," I say. "I'll just watch you."

He says nothing, but I know right away he's thinking, "Weird." He stuffs food into his mouth. When he finishes, he stands and belches and puts on his coat. "Aren't you going to take the leftovers home?" I ask.

He doesn't answer. He leaves money on the table. I follow him out to the car. He's never asked me to dinner since.

I wake in a panic at 4 a.m. There's a bad feeling in my stomach. I get out of bed and dress. It's a two-hour walk to the IGA. It's dark and foggy; everything is still and silent but for the incessant hum of the street lamps in our subdivision. I know that if my father were well, I wouldn't be doing this. I remember the time he came looking for me at the park because it was late and I should have been home. I was talking with friends, and he was carrying his belt. He wasn't going to hit me; he just wanted my friends to think he was. The street lamps were droning then, too, and he pulled me into a bright beam of light and examined my face. "Are you wearing eye make-up?" he asked. His breath was like sweat on my cheek.

I know he won't come looking for me tonight, and I wonder if I'm dreaming. I know that being out this late is crazy. I don't know how I'll explain it to my boyfriend and think, perhaps, once I get to the IGA, I'll hide somewhere and wait until I see him leave, then I'll walk back home. But as I approach the store, he's walking toward me. He asks what I'm doing here. "I just needed air," I say.

On Saturday, he takes me to his house to meet his family. His mother is large and loud and offers me tea. She has an angular face, speaks with an English accent, and presents a succession of questions I can barely keep up with. She flits from subject to subject; talks about her natty dishtowels, Christmas tree ornaments, television programs, and her husband, Teodor, who sits in the living room just beyond the kitchen hatch. "Isn't that so, Dodo?" she shouts.

He's a slight man, nine years her senior and at least six inches shorter than she. He enters the kitchen, peels a banana, and thrusts it in front of my boyfriend's face. "Want a bite?" he asks. He speaks with an Eastern European accent. My boyfriend looks annoyed and wafts the banana away.

His mother calls to his sister, Joanie. She's tall and hunch-shouldered. Her face is like her mother's—the same hooded eyes and

Nubian nose. She slinks into the kitchen, as if she'd been standing by her bedroom door listening and forces a smile. Her teeth are stunningly crooked. She reaches for the teapot, begins pouring cups of tea, and as the remains dribble from the pot into the last cup, she says, "That sounds exactly like Jack going to the bathroom."

I don't know if I'm supposed to laugh. Nobody else does. My boyfriend's mother hands me my cup. Everyone slurps the tea. "What do you think of his highness's hair?" she asks me. My boyfriend has shoulder-length hair. "Everyone thinks he's a girl!" she continues. "How do you think that makes me feel, Jack?"

There's something comforting to me in all of this: no sights or sounds of death exist here, no smells of chemotherapy and disease.

My boyfriend's parents frequently go out, while Joanie, all too often, stays at home. She taps on my boyfriend's bedroom door. "I've just made tea," she says, and sticks her head in. "Hope I'm not disturbing anything." She smiles her crooked-tooth smile as I pull my boyfriend's hand away from my breast and struggle to straighten my sweater. We go to the kitchen where Joanie's pouring. "Sounds like Jack going to the bathroom," she says, intentionally making the tea dribble when she pours my cup.

She tells me she has a Ouija board and that she and her brother and their next-door neighbour, Carol, used to have a lot of fun asking it questions. "Of course, Jack had a crush on her. She was pretty. She had really humongous boobs!"

Joanie pulls three kitchen chairs together and dims the lights. We're all supposed to place the Ouija board on our knees. "Will I get married?" she asks out loud. The plastic pointer flies to the word "Yes." "Who will I marry?" she asks excitedly. The pointer moves to the letter *J* then slowly to the letter *I* and more slowly still to the letter *M*.

"Could that be Led Zeppelin's guitarist, Jimmy Page?" she asks. The pointer flies to "Yes."

"I knew it," she says.

Neither my boyfriend nor I behave skeptically or ask her if she's pushed the pointer. "Okay," she says, "I have another question. Will Jack get married?"

The plastic pointer sails to "Yes." "And who will he marry?" she asks. The letters *C*, *A*, and *R* are laboriously spelled out.

"Carol?" Joanie asks.

"Yes," the pointer indicates.

"How romantic! The girl next door!" Joanie exclaims.

My boyfriend and I walk home from school together every day. Since my introduction to his family, Joanie has started to accompany us. Now she meets me at my locker during my spare. At school, I feel like a robot. Home life doesn't touch me here. The biggest problem I'm asked to deal with is Joanie's ongoing conflicts with her best friend, Elvira, whom she seems to detest. I don't know why she hates her or why she continues hanging around with her and letting her think they're friends. "Wouldn't it just be kinder to tell her the truth?" I ask.

"I don't want to be kind," Joanie says.

I buy a sterling silver heart charm with my babysitting money and have it engraved with my boyfriend's name, then soldered onto the bracelet he gave me. I lift my wrist and jangle the bracelet when I meet him at his locker. "Look," I tell him, "the guys can't say they don't see your name on me anymore."

"Huh?" he mutters.

"The heart," I show him. I hold it, so he can see.

I already know how to read and accommodate his moods. I know when he's feeling happy and communicative and when he's pissed off. I know right now, for example, that he's annoyed with me, though I'm not certain why. I stop talking. Joanie's waiting for us outside of the school. The sky's grey and the air is bone chilling. The wind shoves crumpled papers, tissues, and plastic bags across the schoolyard and through the streets. None of us says anything as we walk home.

My boyfriend is the only male I've ever known who talks seriously about his own sexuality. He tells me that erections can be embarrassing—that a guy has to watch what he's thinking about all of the time. He tells me that the boys swim naked in the pool during gym, that the teacher says it's more hygienic than wearing bathing suits, and that once one of the guys had an erection while standing in line and the other guys laughed at him.

He talks to me about virginity and says he thinks it's important for girls. He says he likes to masturbate. He knows some people say masturbation will make you go blind or insane, and he was worried about this happening to him at first, but he's talked to other guys who do it, and nothing bad has happened to them. He introduces me to the term *wet dream*—"All guys have them," he says. He tells me about the first wet dream he had. He tried to wipe his sheets up with a kitchen dishcloth, but the slick mess just kept spreading. I'm both fascinated and appalled by the things he says; both curious and embarrassed to the point of revulsion. I don't know how he can speak of these things—even the thought of telling him about such private matters makes my stomach sick.

When I'm at school, I look up the word *circumcision* in the dictionary. It's a word I've heard my boyfriend use on several occasions. He told me that he's the only guy in his gym class who's not circumcised, and that makes him feel a little weird, but also kind of special. The dictionary says circumcision is a Jewish practice, and our school is packed with Catholics, so I think he must be wrong and worry that maybe his penis is deformed. It's not so much the ugliness of a deformed penis I worry about, but rather my boyfriend's ability to father a child—to father our child, to be exact, and when I think this, I realize, for the first time, that I expect my boyfriend and I will eventually get married and have a family. I've never thought of myself as a wife or mother before; in fact, in the past I've resisted any suggestion that this might one day be the case. Now, however, I'm thinking I'll marry him, and if his deformed penis causes sterility, we'll just adopt children.

I'm surprised to discover Joanie standing directly behind me. "What word are you looking up?" she asks, craning to see.

"Circumscribe," I stammer, reading the first word my eyes fall on.

"Sounds like circumcise," Joanie says loudly and laughs.

My father is stretched out across the orange couch, sleeping. His face is gaunt and grooved with deep lines. He's covered with a knitted afghan, and the bones of his hips protrude.

The house is so dark and silent, it feels as if death has already arrived. I think about death as a spirit and see in a shadow the outline of a horse rearing over my father's head. I'm afraid to walk past it; to allow my shadow to touch it. I inch along the farthest wall to avoid it before escaping out the front door

I arrive at my boyfriend's house. His parents are out. Joanie waves a tampon pamphlet in front of his face. He'd asked her earlier about the precise location of the vagina. Only just now has she thought of giving him this helpful visual aid.

The phone rings and my boyfriend answers. While he speaks, Joanie pokes her index finger into the ass of his jeans. He swats at her playfully, ineffectually. He turns, winding around and around in the phone's cord. They make faces at each other. They stick out their tongues. They seem as if they'll continue this bizarre game forever, then Joanie says abruptly, "I *have* to see a movie with Elvira. I hope I can make it through the picture without killing her. She's such a downer, always saying she's depressed...depressed, depressed, depressed...If she says that one more time, I'm going to yank her tongue out and cram it up her hole."

It's been a long time since my boyfriend and I have been alone in his house. He turns off the lights and puts on the Olivia Newton John album. I've bought a new bra, one that's padded and has metal hooks and eyes at the back, and I've trained myself not to push his hand away when he fumbles to undo it. I imagine I'm someone else, and it works pretty well until he asks me to take my clothes off. I know he looks at *Penthouse* and *Hustler*. Sometimes he even lifts a copy from work and brings it home, but he says he's curious to see what a real girl looks like naked. I can't bring myself to do this. I try to make a joke out of it. "But I'm not 'a real girl.' I come from the planet Feldspar."

"It's no big deal," he says. "I'm not asking for sex."

"I know," I say, even though I don't know, and it is a big deal to me.

"Look," he says, "I'll take my clothes off." He stands from the bed and starts stripping. He drops his shirt, then his pants. It's dark in the room, but I can see the clothing fall. I'm embarrassed and strangely fearful and suddenly aware that my bra is still undone. I struggle to hook it together. I shut my eyes. I don't want to see him naked because I'm uncertain how I'll respond. I've only ever seen a man's penis in real life once—my father's, when he was hurrying to the bedroom from the shower and his towel dropped. It was shocking to me. It looked nothing like the tiny, porcelain-white penises in the art books I'd looked at. My father and I both pretended nothing had happened, but I couldn't look at him for days.

"Open your eyes," my boyfriend says.

Although my eyes are closed, I know that he's switched the main light on.

"I can't believe you," he says.

I try to open my eyes a little at a time. He's posing by the door, entirely naked, but for a pair of black socks on his feet, and an issue of *Circus* magazine covering his penis. I laugh and he flicks the lights off again, poses on a chair, with his penis hidden beneath a crossed leg, then flicks the lights on. His chest and arms are puny and as white as paper. He's gangly and his shoulders roll forward like a child's. He's making funny poses to amuse me, but I think, even without these poses, the surprise of how vulnerable his body looks makes me want to weep with laughter. I'm glad he's posing, so I can laugh without embarrassing him; I'm also glad that he normally wears clothes. He flicks the lights off again, and we hear his parents walking up the porch steps. He flicks the lights on. I quickly close and cover my eyes with my hands. He scrambles to dress. I negotiate myself to standing. His mother taps on his bedroom door. "We're home, Jack," she says, poking her head in, just as he fastens the last button on his shirt.

I watch the minute hand of our living room clock as my father removes his gauze dressing. The air fills with the stench of shit and decay, and he gags. I open the front door, let in the winter breeze. Snow flutters from the night sky like fat white moths, blows on my eyelashes, and remains there until I blink.

I don't want my boyfriend to come into the house. I don't even want him to come up the porch stairs. I fear my father will invite him in, give him the third degree, make him wonder why he's dating me. My father's hand trembles as he smoothes a new dressing over his abdomen. He pulls his red-check blanket over his chest and shivers from the cold. I see the headlights of my boyfriend's car at the end of the street. "Going now, Dad. See you later." I zip my boots up—push my arms into my coat. I try to get out the door fast before he makes a request: chilled fruit, a foot massage, a different channel on TV. I feel guilty abandoning him, but I know in the next few minutes my mother will walk through the living room and give him what he needs.

When I enter that dark space in my boyfriend's car, I don't care where we drive as long as we drive away, down the bleak court, out of this subdivision, far from the odour of death. There's no reason to share these thoughts with him, no reason to be a downer. I feel so happy when we're driving. I slide close to him and he drops an arm over my shoulder. He does this tonight, just like always, but it feels different and I know something's wrong. We've been together long enough that I have a good idea of how our conversation will go. I'll ask him what's the matter and he'll resist telling me, but eventually if I persist through his annoyance, he'll confide.

We're in the parking lot of Devonshire Mall when he tells me that his father came home drunk, his parents argued, his mother cried. He told his father to leave his mother alone. His father yelled at everyone and said he was going to leave for good, but Joanie cried and held their father's hand and begged him not to, so he didn't. My boyfriend tells me all of this in a monotone. His eyes are fixed and frozen pools. I want to comfort him. I want to tell him everything will be okay, but mostly I want to tell him how much worse things could be. I want to tell him about the shadow of death over my father's head, and the way shit oozes out of his surgical incision that will never heal. I want to tell him what it's like, every day, watching someone you thought was so strong getting weaker and weaker until he can't even lift a spoon. But I don't say these things. I think them, and we sit, deadened and contained, in the silent darkness.

The snow has finally stopped falling, but the streets are filled with it—dirty, white pastry crust that cracks and crumbles under feet; that car wheels pick up like rolling pins and fling into the air. My father is taken to the hospital. Two men carry him down the porch stairs on a kitchen chair. He doesn't know he's dying; that this will be the last time he'll leave the house.

I put my coat on and go outside. Angels of mist rise from my exhalations. It's Saturday, and I don't know where I'll go. I walk to the park, then to the hills by the projects. Finally, I decide to go over to my boyfriend's house, even though I know he'll be leaving for work. I walk quickly, not wanting to miss him. I don't know what I'll say when I arrive.

"What are you doing here?" he asks. I can tell by his tone he's furious.

I don't know what to say at first. Finally, I stammer, "I was just in the neighbourhood." I turn, scuttle down the porch steps, and walk back home.

I walk up the driveway toward my house. I don't want to go inside. It's snowing again, and I stand on the porch staring at the leafless plum tree in our front yard. I see my father being carried away on the kitchen chair. It's like a record skipping or like a film that won't advance—over and over and over again, he's taken away.

I walk down the driveway. Snow continues falling—white cotton wool on wounds—my feet opening new tracks, skidding over ice.

I take the bus to the Metropolitan Hospital. A ten-storey tower is in the process of being built—a hospital addition that, when complete, will house over four times as many beds as the current building does. Beige snow lines the roads outside. Inside, my father's head lolls on a pillow. "That man in the bed across the room," he whispers, pointing to someone who's covered his head with a sheet and makes a creepy mechanical sound. "Cancer of the larynx…terminal…poor devil." My father doesn't know that it's only the morphine that makes him feel well. There are palm trees growing at his feet; his bed is a raft in the South Pacific. "At this rate, I should be home by Christmas," he tells me. Christmas is just over two weeks away.

I play along with his self-deception. It's easy because I deceive myself, too. I laugh at his jokes, take a sip of his dinner—a triple-thick milkshake he can't swallow. He hasn't been this lively in months.

It's only at home that the fantasies fade. In the presence of his orange couch, I'm aware that he's receiving no treatment, that he's given morphine whenever he asks, that he's on a terminal cancer ward, and that he can't even choke down a milkshake.

It's late, but I need to walk somewhere. I call my boyfriend. Joanie answers. "Jailbait on the line," I hear her laugh and whisper before he takes the phone.

"Can I come to your house?" I ask.

"I'll meet you in the park," he says.

"Okay," I say, trying to read his tone.

Air and snow bite my hands and cheeks. He's already in the park. I go to him, plunge my hands inside his pockets, and feel him pull away.

"I don't want to go out with you anymore," he says. "I need to be free. I don't want to feel guilty when I look at other girls."

I'm surprised at what he says, but more surprised by the words that break from my lips, more surprised that I feel no pain or envy. "Just stay with me until my father dies." It's a ridiculous request and I don't know why I ask it. I've said nothing to him about my father's illness. It shouldn't surprise me in the least when he says "No," but it does. It shocks and confounds me, and I can't stop myself from babbling and pleading for him to reconsider. My father is dying. He's not expected to live beyond the week. I tell my boyfriend this, but it doesn't make a difference.

The snow has melted and turned to ice. Everything appears as if it's been encased in glass: the plum tree in our front yard, streets and driveways, cars. I walk to my boyfriend's house. I crawl under the back porch and wait to hear his footsteps. I've never heard the word *stalker*— but a stalker is what I've become. Before he broke up with me, I'd bought Christmas presents for him: albums he'd asked for, clothes that he liked. On the day that my father falls into a coma, I wrap all of these gifts up in bright paper and deliver them to his door.

His house smells of pine, cookies, rum, and cinnamon. There are bowls of chocolates and happy decorations everywhere: reindeers and

Santas, small wooden sleighs, red bows, and jingle bells. He's out, but his mother and Joanie offer me tea.

"Just because you're not dating Jack anymore doesn't mean you have to stop coming over," his mother says. "I know Joanie would like to be your friend."

Joanie smiles and nods.

I walk back home. I walk around the block. I walk to the park. I finally decide to take a bus to the hospital. Visiting hours are over, but a nurse says I can stay as long as I want.

My father's face has become unrecognizable; its shape, its contours, the dry white spit that crusts around his wasted lips. I sit in the chair by his bedside, then stand. I walk through the quiet, brightly lit corridors of the hospital pretending that I'm somewhere else. I imagine myself as another person, as someone chic and beautiful, and toss my hair over my shoulders, just like those confident young women do in shampoo commercials. The gleam from the tiles on the hospital floor becomes stage lights, and when I return to my father's ward and look out his window, I see my role as clearly as I see my hollow-eyed reflection and the hard silver hearts of snow that melt as they plummet to the earth.

He dies, ironically, in "World Population Year," when four billion people inhabit the planet. He dies the year Gerald Ford becomes president, and pardons Nixon for any crimes he may have committed in office, then starts a conditional amnesty for Vietnam draft dodgers. He dies the year *People* magazine makes its debut, and the year the wife of Canada's prime minister, Margaret Trudeau, tells the world she's spent ten days in a psychiatric hospital. He dies the year Patty Hearst is kidnapped and photographed robbing a bank, brandishing an assault rifle, and the year George Foreman and Muhammad Ali vie for the heavyweight championship in the Congo. He dies the same year that fifty per cent of those who've received treatment in North America for the type of cancer he has will survive.

The world will continue, though it's difficult to believe. For me, it's as if an arctic snow has settled, as if I've fallen so deeply asleep that I'll never wake again. In the years to come, I will consider all that coalesced to darkness—the gully into which I fell—the crisis in the time of crisis, and the way my mind and body stayed alive by shutting down.

As a fourteen-year-old somnambulist, stumbling through a handful of waking hours, I lack introspection. I babysit; drop in on people who'd rather I stayed home; trudge a mile and a half to the corner store for cigarettes that must be smoked in secret. When my father is interred, it will almost be Christmas: a holiday that I already associate with grief and disappointment—with feuds and family theatrics, with alcohol, illness, and tyranny. Our artificial Christmas tree stands beside my father's couch, which still smells of pus and feces from his seeping incision. I do not know who assembled the tree. There is a smattering of lights and decorations, but in spite of this, it is bleak and cheerless.

The year before, my brother said that the comet Kohoutek would destroy the earth on Christmas Day. When I looked at the tree, then, I'd unconsciously rip the flesh off my thumbs, hoping for salvation. Now, in the wake of this unexpected destruction, I hope for a blazing comet to smash through our roof—to ignite this Christmas tree, and burn away the poison and monotony of all this misery. My Christmas wish is that my life will end—that those few hours, each day, that I am forced to walk upon the world, will cease. That my memory will evaporate. That I will turn to silver dust.

AFFLICTIONS

I'M FINDING IT DIFFICULT TO BREATHE. I tell my mother I'm taking a bus. I don't tell her, *a goddamned Greyhound bus*. I'm fourteen years old. I don't swear out loud—especially not at my mother. I don't tell her, *It won't cost you a penny, you skinflint*. I don't say, *Considering all the free babysitting I do for you, the least you could do is buy me a bus ticket*. Instead I tell her, as calmly as I possibly can, "I saved the money from *paying* babysitting jobs."

It is April 1975, and in Saigon, thousands are desperate to flee. A Vietnamese economist has tried to sell his pregnant wife to an American, a doctor has forged US passports for his family; others, with no hope, have gone to drugstores, have purchased sleeping pills and tranquilizers with the intent to die. I don't know this. I don't read newspapers. If I've seen it on TV, it hasn't registered. I know, however, that death is sometimes preferable to living.

In my bedroom, I pack cheesecloth peasant shirts, satin smocks, patched and fraying jeans. My mother knows better than to try to stop me from going. There's nothing she can say. I pack my hairbrush, my Jesus sandals made from the hide of water buffalo. They smell of oil and feel like paraffin. Many of the clothes I dress in are Indian imports. I am not aware that girls younger than myself have made them—that some Indian children, as young as five, are sold into slavery for less than thirty dollars, or are simply taken as payment for their fathers' debts. I pack my purple velvet platform shoes and a bar of yellow soap that is shaped like a lemon. But I stop packing when my mother opens my door and tells me she's going out.

I can feel my lungs start burning. I know better than to say, *What the hell right do you have, barging in without knocking?* I know better than to threaten, *Don't you dare pull any of this shit with me.* I zip my suitcase shut, mumble, in an exhalation that sounds like a gasp, "Okay." I am fourteen, and the voice in my head, while crazily screaming obscenities, is sane enough to remain there. If I keep my cool, if I bite my tongue, there is no reason she will be able to manufacture to stop my leaving.

I take my brother's hand. He is happy, but he stutters to the point of unintelligibility. The only thing we really understand is when he says "No." Nine days before he was born, fifteen "war babies" arrived in Canada for adoption. If this was reported on television, I didn't see it. I have no more idea than my two-year-old brother that an India–Pakistan war occurred. It will be years before I learn that Pakistani soldiers raped an estimated three hundred thousand Bengali women and that many of these women became pregnant. I don't know that a nun named Mother Teresa exists or what an abortion really is, and I have not yet heard the word *infanticide*. George Harrison is the closest I come to knowing anything about India's tragedies. I am familiar with some of his music, but ultimately, he is too uncharismatic to interest me. I am vaguely aware of the *Concert for Bangladesh*, though I have no idea what Bangladesh is. I know the word has something to do with India, and it makes me think of golden bangles and sandalwood incense and the musical *Kismet*.

I love my brother and don't mind looking after him, but I resent my mother's total lack of regard for me. I resent the way she doesn't hear me; the way she snoops into my personal possessions and threatens to throw me out or have me locked up for the things she imagines. I resent the way she is intentionally destroying all of my father's belongings and frittering away his life insurance money. She has purchased so many pieces of new furniture and amassed such an array of kitchen gadgets that they can't all fit into our house. "When he was alive, he wouldn't let me buy anything," she complains, "but now he's dead, I can please myself." And she pleases herself by shopping. She buys clothing that she never wears: multiple pantsuits, sweaters, and shells all identical in style, different only in colour. She buys cheap matching jewellery, dozens of plastic beads and earrings, matching shoes and purses, both a coat and a jacket for every day of the week. She carries an Avon catalogue around with her and has every shade of lipstick, eye shadow, and nail polish the company makes. She has every fragrance of Avon cologne and every matching body lotion—Topaze, Foxfire, Ariane—and not just one bottle: she collects all of the specialty decanters.

"I shop therefore I am" is just one of a number of bastardizations of Descartes that have not yet found their way onto bumper stickers, and it will be decades before "Shop till you drop" has become a national motto. I've never heard of *retail therapy, shopaholism,* or *oniomania,* a term coined in 1915 and later included with kleptomania and pyromania as an "impulse insanity."

There is no such thing as compulsive shopping disorder, and the "Yale–Brown Obsessive Compulsive Scale—Shopping Version" has not yet been invented as a psychological indicator. No one has yet done studies showing that between two and eight per cent of the North American population suffer from compulsive shopping, that it often occurs with other psychiatric disorders, and that the antidepressant Citalopram can be helpful in alleviating symptoms.

My mother leaves me to babysit, so she can go to the mall. My heart is racing, my hands are sweating, and my breathing seems to have stopped, but the voice inside my head is calmly saying, *What will you do without me, bitch?* The following morning, when I board the Greyhound, I realize that I'm worrying about my brother. I'm afraid that no one will look after him properly. It is April 1975, and difficult to find reliable childcare. Although Trudeau appointed a child care advisor last year and this decade is one that will witness a ten-to-fifteen per cent increase annually in the number of daycare centres, non-working women like my mother have come to depend on family members, neighbours, and untrained strangers to babysit.

It's a five-hour journey by bus to Toronto, and all the way there I'm trembling and twitching and feeling light-headed. The babysitter my mother hired, before my father died, was a young single woman, a widow, with a small son of her own. When my brother was in his crib and her boy was playing with my brother's toys, she would work on her novel. She believed she would write a bestseller and thought it was the greatest perk that there was a typewriter in our house. When my mother discovered bruises on my brother's legs and bottom, she stopped calling the babysitter. She didn't even ask her to explain; she just never phoned her again. Instead, she started keeping me home from school. Sometimes mornings, sometimes afternoons, and then eventually entire days. "School is pretty bloody useless, anyway," she'd say. Perhaps this was the only thing my mother and I might possibly have agreed upon—if she hadn't added, "for girls."

It is April, and I am travelling to Toronto to visit my friend, Jo, and get away from this suffocation. I have never heard of Shaken Baby Syndrome, although the label has been around since 1971. I have no knowledge of places like Mount Cashel Orphanage in St. John's, Newfoundland, or any number of residential schools where children have been sexually, physically, and emotionally abused. It is 1975 and physical discipline is still practised in the majority of Canadian schools. It is still commonly held that to spare the rod will spoil the child. Adults are predisposed to believe other adults, and not to believe children, so even if my brother didn't stutter, even if he could be clearly understood, it is unlikely that my mother would believe anything he told her.

Your imagination is running away with you; you're like the little boy who cried wolf; don't tell tales. These are the things I imagine her saying to him because these are all things she has said to me.

You idiotic moron. You asshole! the voice inside my head rails, taking my breath away. Even when I'm miles away from her, I cannot stop blaming my mother for being who she is, though I don't know, in any sense, who that might be. I can't stop blaming my mother for not protecting me, for not being wiser, for not being able to love.

Jo is waiting for me at the bus stop on Bay Street. It has been two years since her father went to prison for armed robbery, and her stepmother sent her away. She was my best friend and used to live across the street. Now, she has grown tall and her body womanish. Her hair has grown blonder and longer. Like me, she wears eye make-up, blush, and lip gloss. But she does not look natural in it. She looks like a child dressed up.

I descend the bus stairs, wondering how to greet her. I am startled when her arms embrace me, when she begins singing her variation of the Glad Bag jingle in her goofy voice: "Oh, Mad, we're glad…" She is excited to see me, and I her. I look around, expecting to see her mother also. Last night, her mother called to convince my mother I would be no trouble. She called to let my mother know that I was expected, and, therefore, I must arrive. My mother couldn't argue. She felt cowed by a demanding adult.

"It was pure bullshit," Jo says. "My mother's been gone for weeks." She pulls a package of Export A's from her blouse pocket and offers me one. "My friend, Donna, called." She lights up and takes a hard drag, "My mother's on a toot. We won't be seeing her in the next little while."

I have never heard the word *toot* and imagine it must be a train, but will not ask Jo for fear of demonstrating my ignorance. The bus driver unloads the bags from under the bus, and I collect mine. Jo takes the bag from my hand and slings it over her strong shoulder. "Follow me," she says.

Although it is April, there is snow on the ground. Flurries of dusty white powder swirl in the wind. I follow Jo to a stoplight, over a busy street, under a bridge, and up a long gritty path. For a moment, I do not think of my mother or brother. The voice in my head subsides. I watch the vapour of my exhalations vanish into the cold afternoon.

White doughnut sugar falls from the sky; the moon is a crust of nail, and the cars sound like chainsaws, though I've never in fact heard the sound a chainsaw makes. Jo asks: "How do you escape from a locked room with nothing but a desk and a mirror?"

I don't know.

"You look in the mirror, see what you saw, take the saw, cut the desk in half; two halves make a hole, and you climb out."

We walk along pavement, beside wide black roads, over bridges. I notice a chain-link fence, a tall building, a resilient tuft of weed. There are candy wrappers, chip bags, and fast food serviettes nestled in the icy grass. I remember a time when I could not throw garbage like this away; a time when I would collect it in large plastic bags, hide it just beyond the attic's oblong entry in my closet's ceiling. "Nobody loves you," I'd think. Here, the garbage roams free, ignores relentless traffic, suicidally crosses roads. It is 1975. Woodsy Owl is already four years old, and we've known for over a decade that "Every litter bit hurts." Still, there is more garbage here in Toronto than one should reasonably expect.

Jo carries my case over her shoulder as if it weighed nothing. Our hands are naked, and the sun is sinking into snow. We cross a busy street when I ask, "Do you live very much farther?" Jo says, "Not too," pulling me with a lasso of invisible words, past bleak tarmac, past fine ice dust, past metal posts.

At the bus depot, I anticipated a round-faced mother with a

station wagon, one who would call us "you kids" and offer to stop for milkshakes on the way home—a mother unlike my own. Then I thought maybe a friend of a friend, someone with a car, a helpful neighbour. But there's no one but me and Jo, Jo and me, just the way we used to be.

I don't know how to hitchhike, but she tells me "Just stick out your thumb."

Our thumbs, like frozen cherries, extend from the numbness of our hands, while Fords, Chryslers, and Chevrolets become shadowy smudges, bleeding into the night. I know not to take rides from strangers. I know that strangers are not to be trusted, yet when the black Impala stops for us, I do not hesitate to get inside. The song on the radio is "Radar Love." The driver, tall and thin, nervously taps his steering wheel. He is at least twice our age. He wears a wedding band. I think, *We could beat the crap out of him, if we had to.*

I do not know about Ted Bundy, who, as we take this ride, could be travelling this stretch of road. It will be months before he is arrested in Utah, and years before he is put to death for raping, torturing, and murdering women. Deborah Harry, singer for Blondie, will not yet have announced her close call with Bundy to the media, nor would the media be interested, as her first album, *Blondie*, has not yet been released.

The Impala driver flirts with Jo; he asks her if she wants to smoke a joint. She turns and faces me from the front seat, and I notice the way her hair reflects the fading light. It is 1975. The LeDain Commission has already recommended an end to charges for marijuana possession and cultivation. In fewer than thirty years, the Canadian Medical Association will estimate that 1.5 million Canadians smoke pot recreationally, and Canada will be the first country in the world to legalize marijuana use for the terminally ill.

"Sure, why not," I say, trying to sound as if I smoke pot all the time.

"Sure," Jo tells the driver.

As the car fills with thick, sweet smoke and my heart pounds, I consider this strange elating terror, and how often I have felt it with Jo. It is a feeling of being completely alive because, somehow, it is always connected with the fear of dying. The driver will become impaired, weave from lane to lane, grasp at Jo's breast. When he finally finds the brake pedal, after running a red light, Jo will grab my suitcase and we will escape, laughing hysterically. We will run as we've run before, without feeling the fatigue of our bodies or the pain in our legs. We will run and it will feel as if we fly, out into the freezing darkness, like harpies cast from hell.

The first time I recall running like this was in 1971. Instead of going on a field trip, we hid in the school's bathroom, stood on the toilets, so our feet would not be visible in the stalls. We waited until everything seemed quiet, tiptoed through the hallways, then fled past the main office, Jo screaming an obscenity as we noisily exited. We could hear heavy running behind us, the sound of clumping, exhausted legs finally giving up. A year later, we would be running again, this time after Jo had exploded a can of whipping cream in the teachers' lounge of a Catholic school. We'd gotten into the school by sliding a mitten into the frame of an electronically locking door. We'd just wanted to see what the school looked like. They had better facilities than ours—expensive gym equipment, a professional-looking theatre. We played with floodlights and jumped on the trampolines. Then Jo said she was hungry and went foraging in the staff room's fridge. She took two bites out of an apple and offered it to me. I didn't want it, so she threw it on the floor. Then she found the whipping cream and wanted to see what would happen if she smashed the can. The janitor heard us and called the police.

When we got out of the school, it sounded like there were sirens everywhere. We ran past our subdivision, out to the train tracks. The next evening in the paper, there was an article about a break-in at the school. It said there had been some vandalizing and a large sum of money had been stolen. I thought in 1972 that Jo and I had been lucky we did not run into the thief—but in Toronto, I begin to wonder who the thief might actually have been.

At some point, this highway becomes a brightly lit suburban street, and Jo, still breathless, says, "Look what I got!" She pulls a wallet out of her jacket pocket, opens it, and slides out the bills. Then, she closes it, tosses it in a municipal garbage can and announces: "Pizza tonight!"

I don't say anything, just look at her.

"He was a jerk," she says.

I think of the man's greasy hair, his wedding band, the look on his face when he went after Jo. I think, *Somewhere in this city, this man has a wife. He might have a child,* and I see my baby brother's face.

"You shouldn't throw his wallet in the garbage," I tell her. "You ought to put it in a mail box."

"Okay," she says, retrieving the wallet. We spend the next half hour looking for a post box, and afterwards I follow Jo and my suitcase to the doors of a high-rise building. The security intercom doesn't work anymore but hangs from red and blue wires against a brick wall. The elevator has missing buttons; the one Jo presses is upside down. There is a smell of old food, of spices, of starch—a smell of children whose diapers need changing, children who need to be bathed.

"Pakis," Jo says, when we ascend, as if I should understand what she's talking about.

The plastic numbers are missing from Jo's apartment door, and someone has attempted to write them with bright blue magic marker. There is a hole in Jo's apartment wall—a big, round, ragged hole, the kind I will learn much later results from a punch. It contains clothing and shoes and something else I can't quite make out. When I ask Jo about it, she changes the subject.

The living room is sparsely furnished. A small, threadbare couch, a metal floor lamp, a lawn chair. The floors everywhere are covered in the same grey linoleum tile. The kitchen is small and empty. In Jo's bedroom, there is an old grey sleeping bag bunched on the floor, dirty laundry, a necklace, and although I am aware my mother would call this "squalor" and insist I leave, I feel comfortable here in a way I never felt at home.

It is 1975, and I am with Jo in her mother's low-income apartment a few blocks east of Jane and Finch. I will not know the notoriety of this neighbourhood, considered troubled since the early seventies, nor that thirty years from now the *Toronto Sun* will publish a series of articles about gangs, drugs, and guns in this neighbourhood, but with a hopeful slant. They will blame the ongoing problems on bad city planning, overcrowding, and poverty. Some thirty years in the future, statistics will record seventy-five thousand people from more than seventy countries living in this stretch of land.

But in 1975 I am fourteen years old and have no understanding of what a "social problem" is. It will be five years before I return to college as a mature student, take a sociology course, and begin to turn the prism of my history into abstractions. Right now, I am only aware of differences—of sights, smells, and sounds that are strange to my privileged senses. I am only aware of the relaxed feeling in this squalor; of Jo seeming so completely independent, of her embarrassment when she tells me, "We have cucarachas," and, in spite of my embarrassment, I must ask her to tell me what that is.

And the apartment does have "cucarachas"—hundreds and thousands of them that hide in the daytime under the heavy plastic strips that skirt the walls. They hide in the kitchen's cracks and crevices, underneath the stove, inside the dark workings of light fixtures. If there was any food here—boxes of cereal, bags of sugar or rice—they would hide there, but even without these amenities, the "cucarachas" seem to find Jo's apartment—indeed, the whole building—a procreative paradise.

Before now, I had never seen a cockroach and knew nothing of their furtive ways. I was unfamiliar with their gleaming appearance, their stink, the trail of pepper droppings they leave behind. That night, after we eat pizza and prepare to go to bed in her room, Jo tells me that she sleeps with the lamp on. I don't realize the wisdom in this until I venture into the bathroom, flick the light switch on, and see the dark army scatter. "What is it that they do exactly, these cucarachas?" I ask Jo, but she isn't certain.

It will be at least six years before I hear the hypothesis that cockroaches can survive a nuclear war. I will not know that cockroaches can safely withstand the radiation of a thermonuclear explosion, that most poisons can't touch them, and that they can live and reproduce up to a month without heads.

Jo tells me that the cockroaches came from the "Pakis." She says that the "Pakis" tried to make vegetable gardens in their living rooms; that the cockroaches were in the dirt. Before I came to Toronto, I'd never heard the word *Paki*, and although I have been aware of racism for a number of years, in my mind it exists only in the United States and has to do with white and black Americans.

"What is a Paki?" I want to know, thinking of suitcases and bundles on pack mules, but Jo cannot answer with certainty.

It is 1975, and European economies are strengthening. The majority of immigrants coming to Toronto, to Canada, are no longer from the British Isles, and there are no more American draft dodgers. It is four years since Pierre Trudeau first adopted a policy of multiculturalism and two years since the Canadian Multiculturalism Council was set in place. In two years time, the 1977 Citizenship Act will "remove any trace of special treatment for British subjects" in Canada, and some thirty years from now, Toronto will have the highest metropolitan percentage of foreign-born residents in North America.

"Pakis don't know how to live here," Jo says, and I will discover in the days to come that "Pakis," according to Jo, encompass a wide range of immigrants including Vietnamese, Chinese, and people from the West Indies, as well as Pakistan and other East Indian groups.

"The Pakis break things and don't fix them, they don't know how to use a dustpan and broom, they sleep in their outside clothes, they steal, they treat their kids bad." These are the things Jo's mother has told her, and when I meet her, she will tell me the same, after throwing up and before passing out on the living room floor drunk. She does not sleep at the apartment often. She has a number of boyfriends and she usually stays with them. She drops by once a month to pick up her government cheque. She leaves in the morning, before we are awake, and today, Jo will swear and cry because her mother has left no money, only an empty bottle on the kitchen table.

"It's Okay," I try to comfort her. "I brought my babysitting money… I can pay for food."

But there is no bread left, there is no milk left, and there is no Kraft Dinner. The cupboards and refrigerator are completely bare. The cucarachas are eating the paint off the walls; they are eating the oily residue that formed around the kitchen fan from previous occupants; they are eating each other's shit.

"You're supposed to be my guest," Jo says. "I'm supposed to show you a good time." Her nose will be red from crying. Her eyes like two circles of fire. "I wanted it to be nice for you."

I won't be able to convince her that it is nice for me—just being here, just being away from the hell I know—from an angry intrusive mother and the thick grief of a father's death that hangs in our house like the smell of tar. I can't explain how I sleep all day long, as if I had fallen under a curse. And it's not just the words that are missing to explain—but the time and space it will take for me to digest and understand everything I live that makes me unhappy.

That night, we paint our toenails red and dress in platform sandals and satin shirts. We share make-up in the bathroom, cotton candy lip gloss, peaches and cream blush. We paint our eyelids blue and comb purple mascara through our lashes; then we hitchhike downtown.

It is 1975, and there are no such things as "age of majority cards." Three years ago, the legal drinking age dropped from twenty-one to eighteen in Ontario, and the repercussions of serving minors in a bar are not frequently enforced. When Jo lived in Windsor, we'd stand at the liquor store and give men money to buy us tequila. No one ever refused us. And here, in the clubs and bars, no one refuses us either. We both get a bottle of "Blue" and sink into our chairs.

I think we should be conserving money for food, but Jo tells me not to worry about it. The disco music thrums through the soles of our platform shoes and Jo smiles at a man, a plump and dumpy man, at a table beside us. Before I know it, he has joined us, and so has his buddy. His name is Greg; his buddy is Mike. Can they buy us lovely ladies a beer? Jo lets Greg rub his fat thigh against her thigh. She runs her fingers through her hair and licks the cotton candy lip gloss on her lips. Greg and Mike buy us each a bottle of beer, they buy us chicken strips and french fries, and then Greg says he's got to level with us. He says that he and Mike are looking for some action. We could make it a foursome, he says, or "If you lovely ladies prefer, you could do us separately, as long as you do us together because it would really turn us on to watch a couple of girls playing with each other."

I'm watching Jo's face, and seeing some kind of metamorphosis. She is not my fourteen-year-old friend: her eyes have become sharp, her mouth has transformed into a flower, her hand falls on Greg's knee, her blond hair sways like a curtain, and she leans over, pressing her arm against his chest, whispering in his ear.

I feel my face get hot. I want to give the chicken strips and the french fries back. I want to spit the beer onto their shirts to show my disgust and tell them, "Take a fuckin' hike." But Jo has already taken Greg's money. She's folding it in her hand just like a handkerchief, and I think of my father, my dead father, and the white handkerchiefs he wore in his suit pocket every day he went to work.

"We'll be right back," Jo says, rubbing Greg's thigh, standing. She extends her hand toward me. "We need to go to the can and check out the mirror."

She's smiling at me, and it's a smile that says, "Look happy, don't let them see that you're not." It's a smile I know from grade school—the smile she gave me when she copied the answers off my math test. Mrs. Freed, our grade five teacher, accused us of cheating, and Jo told her with complete conviction that we had not. "I saw you," Mrs. Freed insisted. "You leaned right over her chair and she let you see her test." Jo smiled that disarming smile. "I didn't, Mrs. Freed." Even I believed her.

In the bathroom, I tell Jo that I think she's completely crazy. I tell her that I'm not a hooker and there's no way on earth that I'd do anything with these scumball guys, but Jo isn't listening. She's looking intently above my head, toward the ceiling. She sees something, and I don't know what it is, but I'm thinking "cucarachas." Her eyes narrow and she takes a running jump toward the sinks. The same hand she used to take the money removes one of her sandals, and slams it toward a row of frosted windows. "You look in the mirror, see what you saw, take the saw, cut the desk in half; two halves make a hole, and you climb out," she says, smashing a pane of glass clean through.

I scuttle up behind her, onto the sinks, away from the blinding bathroom light and out, through the window frame, into darkness. I have forgotten my past, forgotten my family. I am only aware that the cold night air is hitting my face, and my legs are running without pain or exhaustion. They are running, as if they act reflexively, against my wishes, because they know that I'm completely alive.

FLUSH

I ARRIVED THE YEAR the toilet made its cinematic debut. Moments before the famous murder scene in Alfred Hitchcock's *Psycho*, Janet Leigh, the victim, flushes incriminating evidence down the loo. The first toilet to appear on the silver screen is strikingly white, and the flush strikingly loud. The appearance of this toilet is an indication of advancing times. Three years before, the commercial censors ban an episode of *Leave It to Beaver* because a toilet bowl is shown. In 1960, I have not yet seen *Leave It to Beaver*, know nothing of June Cleaver's princess dresses or her simple string of pearls. In the next few years, I will discover these things, but it will be decades before I understand the significance of the time into which I am born, this great evolutionary leap, this fundamental cultural turning point, and the way it will influence and shape my life. The year I am born is the year in which moving picture meets the appliance of moving bowel.

They say "You can't go back," and although in 1960 I've never heard them say it, I already know my mother's uterus is out of reach to me, the pink, fleshy walls of her womb, the warm sack of fluid where I swam. I have been violently expelled from Eden, a wayfarer, a refugee, set in a cot, fed with a bottle, left to scream. And Janet

Leigh flushes the toilet, and the flush sounds like death, like the first sound a baby hears when she enters the noisy, sordid world. But is the world any more sordid than it ever was? If only I had consulted my omniscience in those first few moments when I may have still been bound with heaven, perhaps I would have learned the reason I chose this moment to be born.

Fast-forward forty-five years: suffering from jet lag in England, unable to read or write, I switch on television. The program *No Angels* is playing. In the first thirty minutes, a drunken man shits his pants; a nurse has sex with a stranger in a car; and a young doctor experiences a premature ejaculation. In Canada, I have not watched TV for years, but I'm certain there's nothing comparable to this. Thirty-two years ago when I lived here, there was the lewd and bawdy *Benny Hill Show, George and Mildred*, and *Man about the House*. Having emigrated from North America, I was shocked by all of these programs with their blatant sexual and earthy content, though today I wouldn't even bat an eye if I saw them in Canada. Television "toilet humour" is what my father would have called it. And if he'd lived long enough to witness it, I imagine, he would have paid me, just as he had done with cigarette commercials, each time I switched such offending programs off.

It may be that Britain signals the shape of things to come for North American TV and cinema (Alfred Hitchcock was born in Leytonstone, London, after all), or it may be that all the continents of the world are on some kind of inevitable slippery slope. The censors refused to pass *Psycho*, not because of the toilet, which was troubling enough, but because Janet Leigh's nipple was visible in the shower scene. Hitchcock didn't edit. He knew they wouldn't review the film again. He lingers in the bathroom, in a coming attraction teaser, gazing at the toilet, a master of suspense. When the white porcelain toilet flushes, the world changes. In Detroit, Michigan, in Crittenton General Hospital, there are women flushing toilets, too.

They have been routinely prepped and given enemas. Some will soon be mothers for the first time; others, like my own, will have been through it all before. Obstetric ultrasound technology is in its infancy, so none of these women will know the sex of their children. The booties they have made and purchased are predominantly yellow. It will be six years before the fetal heart is "interrogated" and found to sound like "horse's hoofs when running" and another year before placental blood flow will be described as "rushing wind." It will be almost eight years before "the human eye pierces the 'black box' of the womb" and eighteen years before it's described this way in the foreword to an international ultrasound symposium proceeding. But in 1960, the human eye has long pierced the "idiot box." Ninety per cent of Americans have TV sets in their homes and watch programs like *Gunsmoke*, *My Three Sons*, and, of course, *Alfred Hitchcock Presents*. In Britain, Granada TV launches *Coronation Street*. This will become the longest-running soap opera in the world and will remain the most popular show in England for over four decades.

Meanwhile, labouring women in North America are anaesthetized and sent into a haze of "twilight sleep"—these procedures numb their bodies, steal their minds, and depress their infants. In 1960 it is better, simply, to forget—to accept amnesia with equanimity and afterwards be wheeled from delivery room to ward, transferred to bed, and remain there, catheterized. Moving picture will not meet the appliance of moving bowel for the new mothers at Crittenton General, at least not yet, as ultrasonic imaging of the unborn has not yet happened, and the paralyzing drugs these mothers have absorbed will prevent anything resembling the natural functioning of bowels. When catheters are finally removed, these invalid mothers will still be bedridden. The only violent flush will be their crimson faces, as nurses slide bedpans under their sheets and encourage them to pee. Hitchcock once said, "The length of a film should be directly related to the endurance of the human bladder," but he said this not knowing the capacity of a mother's traumatized bladder to endure.

The portable television era began four years ago, and more than five hundred television stations are broadcasting in the US, but few of these women have access to sets in the hospital. Instead, once they are mobile, they shuffle to the end of the long corridor, buy cigarettes from the dispensing machines, and painfully perch at the end of waiting room chairs to take in their favourite programs. These include soap operas like *The Edge of Night* and dramas like *Perry Mason*. Knowing the sex of their children now, friends and relatives have procured them appropriate coloured wool, so they can begin knitting gender-specific sweaters for their babies. They will speak to each other about their babies, gossip about other women, and drink prune juice by the gallon. They will watch commercials about Spic 'n Span and Cheer, and think about ways to get their homes, dishes, hair, husbands, laundry, children, pets, and possessions really, really clean. Since the early fifties there has been an obsession with chemical cleanliness. Arrays of diverse cleaning products have mushroomed in the marketplace, and become increasingly specialized. For example, a farsighted company, knowing the toilet is destined to come out of the water closet and need to be cleaned, has purchased Ty-D-Bol this year, but the famous little singing man in a boat, who serenades the goggled-eyed housewife from the bright, blue- tide waters, is only a glimmer in an ad man's eye. In forty-five years, seventy thousand new chemical compounds will have been dispersed into the world, and the Ty-D-Bol sailor moored, in spite of his popularity, and having nothing to do with water pollution. The toilet flushes, and the world changes. We have not yet begun to question the contents of what goes down the drain.

These new mothers at Crittenton General don't speculate. They smoke and chat about the here and now, about the nurseries they have assembled, about in-law problems. The environment consists only of hospital beds, tables and chairs, the pictures of babies on the walls. It is nine years before Time magazine runs its article on the chocolate-coloured Cuyahoga River that has a history of spontaneous chemical combustion, and ten years before the first "Earth Day." In the future, historians will label this time the gold rush of nuclear reactors, when companies such as General Electric, Combustion Engineering, and Westinghouse are bursting to fill the world with the heat and light of nuclear fission, and almost everyone thinks it's a wonderful idea. Three Mile Island is nineteen years in the future, and no one in this hospital has ever even heard of the city of Chernobyl. But in England, there are still people who recall "the days of toxic darkness" when the combination of coal smoke and fog killed over twelve thousand people. There are those who still reflect upon the creepy, insidious nature of this event that stole lives away, without anyone realizing, until undertakers ran short of caskets and florists short on flowers.

But there is no shortage of flowers here: pink roses and carnations announce the birth of daughters; blue irises and delphiniums announce the birth of sons. Arthur Kornberg produced DNA in a test tube in 1957, but the genetic engineering of cut flowers is over three decades away, so all of these bouquets are destined to an early end. Blue carnations have not yet been developed, and although the smell is lovely, the dozen roses my father brings my mother have not yet been engineered to hold their scents.

Although I can't recall, I imagine my sleep is deep and dreamless when my father and his flowers arrive. When I open my eyes, I stare at the nursery ceiling, instead of looking into my mother's bewildered face. I imagine hearing the mid-western accents of the busy nurses, instead of my mother's British lilt. I imagine wondering what the hell I'm doing here. *The Dick Van Dyke Show* is a year away, and the controversial episode in which Rob suspects he and Laura have been given someone else's child in the hospital will not be aired until 1963. Since DNA testing is still the jurisdiction of science fiction, there are no definitive ways to discover answers to questions of mix-ups, or unquestionable questions about paternity. It is still mother who knows best.

These new mothers are submissive in spite of the feminist movement, which is about to explode, and despite Betty Friedan, who is already thinking about "the problem that has no name." They will take the babies they are given, without question, and only later, when these babies reach adolescence, begin to ask themselves what went wrong. Hemorrhoids, episiotomies, and paralyzing drugs make the first bowel movements for these women a torturous experience, far more painful than the contractions of childbirth they cannot recall. The bathrooms in this hospital are small, box-like, cold. The toilets are clinical and high off the ground. Small, fat women like my mother teeter upon them. The room smells like a mixture of chemical disinfectant and urine. If I were to make a film of my life now, I think I would begin it here: a tiny female child, cradled in her mother's arm, hovering over a hospital toilet.

"Drama is life with the dull bits left out," Hitchcock said, but it is more than the dull bits we extract. The General Principles of the Hays Code, which governed motion picture production from 1930 until the year of my birth, stated: "No picture shall be produced that will lower the moral standards of those who see it. Hence the sympathy of the audience should never be thrown to the side of crime, wrongdoing, evil or sin; correct standards of life, subject only to the requirements of drama and entertainment, shall be presented; law, natural or human, shall not be ridiculed, nor shall sympathy be created for its violation."

Forty-three years from the date the Hays Code is defunct, digital formatting will make it easy to create professional-looking movies on a computer. George Lucas will use digital cameras to film the last of the *Star Wars* movies, and a thirty-two-year-old doorman, Jonathan

Caouette, will use his iMovie program, spend just a little over two hundred dollars, and produce an award-winning documentary about his troubled, down-the-toilet past.

If I were to make a film of my life now, I wonder what I would include and what I would cut. Caouette included old videos of life with his mentally ill mother and his eccentric grandparents, of himself in foster care, in drag, in the persona of a battered woman, and as a young gay man throwing up in a toilet after receiving news of his mother's lithium overdose. What he does not include are videos of his son and of the woman he impregnated. He omitted these intentionally because they present aspects of his life out of keeping with its general trajectory.

There are years of my life, between the ages of fourteen and nineteen, that haunt me from the cutting room floor. Like Caouette's omissions, these years are out of sync and do not follow a linear storyline. They drop me in another continent; leave me in a cultural time warp where only the toilet remains constant and true.

The spectre first appears in Cleveland. My five-year-old brother, four years my senior, pulls the channel selector off the television and flushes it down the toilet. The toilet is utterly blocked. My father, unwilling to pay a plumber, will fix it himself. Besides a wicked sense of humour, my father also possesses an eight-millimetre movie camera. He sets it up on a tripod to film this event. In years to come, we will sit in darkness watching my father shut off the water supply, siphon out the tank, remove the nuts that hold the bowl to the floor flange. We've heard the story a hundred times—seen it a hundred more—my father succeeds in removing the blockage. An expression of joy imbues his face. He sets the toilet down on the floor flange. As he moves to secure it, the film catches an alteration. We know what has occurred, though my father does not yet. We know that the toilet bowl has cracked and that the cost of replacing it will be significantly more than a plumber.

Four years after making this movie, my father is in debt, drinking hard liquor, and chain smoking. We travel to Chicago to install an intercom system in our expensive, new house under construction. There are lines and vents of rough plumbing for three bathrooms, but the absence of toilets makes my bladder heavy. My father fiddles with hard square speakers and web-thin cords. I don't want to disturb him. I don't want to risk his rage. But he is not angry when I tell him. He places me on his shoulders, carries me to the dark stairless pit that opens into the basement, and begins to descend a rickety ladder. Although I can't recall where I've seen it, I am thinking of Alfred Hitchcock's movie *Vertigo*—or rather, the word *vertigo*, which I learned as a result of seeing the film. It bombed in 1958 because, some say, it was too dark for the light-craving audiences of *Auntie Mame* and *Houseboat*. Hitchcock once said: "Give them pleasure—the same pleasure they have when they wake up from a nightmare." And that is exactly the kind of pleasure I am experiencing on my father's shoulders, the kind of pleasure that I have already experienced too much of in my life.

Although I am only seven, I already have trouble sleeping at night: I fear the dark, I fear spiders, I fear the invisible monsters lurking beneath my bed and the princess lamp that once violently wobbled, for no apparent reason, on my bedside table. At home, I never fall asleep in bed, but always on a stair leading down into the living room where my parents spend the evening fighting.

As I teeter on my father's shoulders now, I think of my sleeping habits, and wonder how, with such "vertigo," I have managed to survive. When my feet touch clay, my father directs me to a hole in the corner the construction workers made. I am humiliated, disgusted, incredulous. Only twice, so far, since I could use a toilet have I ever experienced not using one. Both times were bad.

Rewind to 1965. There I am in the school ground, playing tag. I need a toilet, but the school doors are locked. I know I should go home, but my brothers aren't ready to leave, and I'm afraid to walk past the ravine alone. I continue playing, trying to forget the overwhelming pressure of my full bladder, hoping my mind can control this. No one is more surprised than I when I wet myself. The kids in the playground laugh. My brothers, mortified, escort me home. My mother gives me a bath and tries to assure me that no one at school will remember, but I know she is wrong. I make her promise to buy me a blond wig, sunglasses, and a bright red sweater. I make her promise to re-enroll me in kindergarten as someone completely new. I will not calm down until she promises, and on Monday, when she does not buy me my disguise and insists I go to school exactly as I am, I know I will never completely trust her again.

Fast-forward to 1966: our car breaks down on a highway. I go into the grassy field behind the car to pee. It is a hot summer day and we have been waiting for a tow truck for an eternity. I am embarrassed, but my parents assure me no one will see. Fast-forward to the day after: my rear end is the colour of a Japanese sun and itches with a potency I have never known. I wonder what curse has befallen me, if I unintentionally touched my private parts while I was sleeping and brought this plague upon myself. I can't bring myself to speak of this, but when the blisters form and break, the pain drives me to my mother who, on examining my backside, summons our family doctor. He diagnoses my condition as poison-ivy related. For the next week, I lie in my bed on my stomach, my ravaged naked bottom on display.

"You can't trust anyone over thirty," Berkeley dissident Jack Weinberg told a reporter in 1964, and although I would not even hear this phrase until I was studying American history at the University of Western Ontario in 1981, something in the collective ethos had infected me. Both of my parents are over thirty when I'm born and they continue getting older. The white porcelain toilet flushes—or it doesn't. The world changes just the same.

My father's drinking keeps him out late, gets him in car accidents, fist fights, and finally an unemployment line. A month later, he gets a job as an *Encyclopaedia Britannica* salesman. This is the year Neil Armstrong lands on the moon. His small step is one giant leap for mankind, while my father's small step drags him around our affluent neighbourhood. Nobody's hungry for knowledge. He can't give encyclopedias away. It's 1969, the *Saturday Evening Post* stops its presses after 147 years, The Beatles record their last album, and Paul McCartney is rumoured dead. Charles Manson and his followers kill Sharon Tate, Nixon succeeds Johnson, and *The Brady Bunch* and *Sesame Street* make their network debuts.

On Christmas day, we move from our large, beautiful house to a small, shabby one in Windsor. My brothers share a bedroom and we all have to share one toilet. This would not be half so bad if my father did not have chronic constipation. He spends a large percentage of his time, when he's home, in the bathroom reading books on World War II. When he's not in the bathroom, he's in the basement, smoking and drinking and building a bar. There are no corporate rehabilitation programs, and although some health professionals view it as such, the vast majority do not consider alcoholism a disease. Every middle-class home has a wet bar. Cocktail hour begins at five. The only hope for a person like my father is to start a business of his own and to run it into the ground.

Fast-forward to 1974. I am drunk and kneeling over a toilet at the Fire Side Inn restaurant at my father's funeral reception. Two hours earlier, my father was interred in the mausoleum at Green Lawn Cemetery, the same place his father was interred in 1961 and his mother will be interred in 1983. The year my father dies is three years after Dr. Denis Burkitt publishes the results of his study comparing diet and the incidence of colon cancer in North America and Africa, and brings the term *fibre* into common usage. It is three years after it has become stylish to eat bran cereals for breakfast and to bring raw broccoli and carrot sticks to parties as finger food. In years to come, there will be passionate debates about the role of dietary fibre in cancer prevention, but right now, fibre seems to be a preventative panacea, and my father never liked eating high-fibre foods. It has not yet been postulated that cigarette smoking and alcohol increase the incidence of this cancer, nor that fat and lack of exercise are extremely unhealthy "lifestyle choices." In fact, the concept of lifestyle choices is new and has not yet been exploited by weight loss businesses or dismissed by economists. In years to come, the colon will become the third most common site for cancer, and in thirty-one years, an estimated 104,950 new cases of colon cancer will be diagnosed in the United States alone.

But right now, as I lean over the toilet, I see my father. I am not thinking of his unhealthy lifestyle, or his bowel obsession, which began with his constipation several years ago. I am thinking of his split personality, his dichotomy, the kind, sober him and the mean drunk. I am projecting into the future and wondering how I will ever be able to reconcile the past. What kind of person was he? What was my experience of him? What will I choose to remember and what will I choose to flush away?

The year I am born, Jack Parr walks off the *Tonight Show* because the NBC censors edit out a segment in which he tells a joke about a toilet. The joke is innocuous—about travellers in England looking for a wayside chapel, and seeing a sign announcing "W.C." Parr doesn't even say the words "Water Closet." For weeks, newspapers carry stories about this national controversy. Things will never be the same.

Fourteen years later, some kind of amnesia falls over me. I awake in England, or at least partially awake. My mother, in her panic, has sold, given away, or burned everything we owned in Windsor and has moved to England. She has had to make major decisions about what to take with her and what to leave behind. She has decided that my father was a terrible bastard and that she's well rid of him. She has had to throw out her entire life in North America as bad business, to return to the place of her birth and the home of her brother and sister-in-law. Because I am fourteen, she takes me with her. Everything is different here: the accents, the currency, the electrical outlets. In 1974 the school system in England is impenetrable to a North American high school student; there are no equivalencies, no opportunities of entry. One night, my aunt tells me she's found a job for me, and the next day, I begin working in a hotel as a chamber maid. I clean toilets every day of my life, toilet after toilet, for the next five years, until the white porcelain toilet flushes and I decide to make a final cut.

HACKING

IT STARTED WITH A KIND OF TREMOR, deep in the back of my throat, a tickle, a tingle that wouldn't go away. I flushed the toilet, held my breath, sprinkled in the magic blue crystals. They left a nimbus of powder swirling in the air. I stuck my naked hand into the bowl. Sylvia, who had trained me, said it was the only way to get the toilet really clean. "See all the little pieces of shit come loose?" She swished her own white terry cloth rag around and then shoved it down into the place where the porcelain curved. "Filthy buggers!" she said, attacking it again.

I wasn't sure if she was talking about the flecks of swimming shit or the former inhabitants of this room, two ancient ballet dancers, who, I was told, came every winter and joined the curtain panels together with pins. The windows looked out onto the ocean. Downstairs, in the stillroom, we speculated about their sunless boudoir, and the anxious way they chanted, "Someone's at the door!" every morning when we knocked to bring them tea.

"Can I use gloves?" I asked Sylvia.

"Gloves," she said.

"Yeah, you know, plastic gloves,"—the yellow kind, I thought, the kind my mother used to use when she dyed her hair.

"What? You think you're the bloody queen? You think the flesh God gave you is any different than these little buggers?" She was talking about the flecks of shit. I stuck my bare hand in the next toilet. After a while, it stopped bothering me. But what was bothering me now was my cough. I was coughing and coughing. Coughing so loud and hard that the hotel guests stopped in the corridors and stared.

I lived in the very top floor, in the very top room, of the Candar Hotel in Ilfracombe, North Devon. Ilfracombe was a town that depended on tourists in the spring and summer, and the dole the rest of the year. When I first got the job as a live-in chambermaid, before I had the cough, I bought a second-hand wooden kitchen table from a travelling auction and carried it all the way up the high street. The street was narrow and so steep it seemed perpendicular (thus "high," I presumed). Two skinny pavements flanked it, and when it rained, which was often, they became as slick as snot. This, I was told, had something to do with the seaside environment and the moss. The crepe soles on my work shoes couldn't make it up the street unless I ran. Otherwise, for every step I took, I'd slide back three.

Yorkshire Ann wanted to know what I needed the kitchen table for. She was a pixie-faced woman with dark, curly hair. She was in her thirties but barely looked as if she'd hit puberty. She'd left her mum and her numerous siblings to come down to Ilfracombe with her boyfriend, George, and work the season.

"I'm going to write a book," I told her. "I need a table for my typewriter." I had a blue-and-white manual typewriter. I'd rescued it from my mother's Pickford crate the day she moved back to Canada.

"What kind of book are you wanting to write, then?" Yorkshire Ann asked. She was very curious and very direct. "Smut?"

The truth was, I hadn't really thought about what I wanted to write. I figured if I sat with my hands on the typewriter keys long enough, some story would find its way through the tips of my fingers.

"It's been a long time since I've had a really good read of smut," she said. "Some Sundays, on an evening back home, me Mam and me, and our Cora and our Mary and our Doris, we'd all read smut together, round the fire." Her eyes got glassy whenever she talked about home. "We took turns reading, and mam would be busy fussing with knitting, and whenever we'd get to a good bit, Mam would start dropping stitches and say, 'See what you made me do now!'"

"Maybe I'll try to write a memoir," I said.

"You're too young for that," she said. "You've barely had any life yet. Wait a bit. It's smut that sells. You could get rich writing smut. Smutty romance! That's what you want to be writing."

I considered what she said. For a moment, I saw myself lounging next to a built-in swimming pool, notebook and pen in hand, decked out in a feather-trimmed champagne peignoir.

"Can you type quickly, then?" Anne asked, sailing on to her next thought and amputating my fantasy.

I'd taken touch-typing in high school before I'd dropped out. My fingers used to fly over the electric keyboard of the school's Olivetti machine. Our teacher, Mrs. Hooper, taped a piece of paper over our hands so we couldn't cheat. She'd make us type for sixty seconds, and then she'd grade what we typed. For every error we made, she'd deduct two points. Then she'd add those numbers and subtract them from sixty. I ended up with a score of negative twenty. I soon realized I'd get better marks on my typing tests if I just sat at my desk and did nothing.

"Kind of fast," I told Ann.

"If you're clever enough to type, why aren't you working in an office, then? Working in an office with a nice, handsome boss?"

My mother wanted me to be a secretary. She even said she'd loan me the money to go to a business college and learn to type properly. My auntie Lena also thought I should become a secretary, but, for her, a business college wasn't a prerequisite. "Go on the continent as a shorthand typist, bluff your way through."

"I'm not that clever," I told Ann.

When I had fit the table under the little dormer window in my room, I covered its stained and ugly top with sticky contact paper; then I set my typewriter on top. Every day after work, I tried to do a little writing: the first three paragraphs of a murder mystery; two-hundred-and-fifty words of science fiction; the tentative hook for a feature-length article for *Look* magazine; a rhyming poem that could be turned into lyrics for a Roger Whittaker contest; but my energy dissipated quickly, and I usually ended up gazing out the window, communing with the seagulls.

Our head housekeeper, Mrs. Newell, spoke the Queen's English and chain smoked Woodbines. She'd been a WREN during the war, and constantly let it be known that she had very, very high standards of cleanliness. She also had one walleye that terrified everyone when they first met her. "What you really need is a method in your madness," she told me when I mentioned my writing problems. "You need to choose one project and stick to it, and force yourself to write the same number of words every day."

For Mrs. Newell, method was everything. This philosophy, along with an ironclad will and a passion for discipline, was born from her training in the navy, and, unlike the rest of us regular maids, she did possess a pair of gloves—but not the plastic kind. Her gloves were the white cotton military sort, and she donned them at the end of each working day before straddling dangerous stair railings and sometimes crawling up twenty-foot ladders to place her index finger on a light fixture.

"Dust!" she'd exclaim, returning to her point of departure and sending one of us maids on an immaculate mission, to be suspended someplace in the sky, yellow shammy in motion.

"Don't look down!" she'd sing in her sweet refined voice, as polished with elocution as the objects of our toil were with Pledge.

"Fine work!" she'd commend when we completed the task. "Good lass."

I liked being Mrs. Newell's "good lass" and generally found her advice on most matters excellent. So with new determination I returned to my garret and forced myself to doggedly churn out two typed pages a day. I settled on completing the mystery, since I needed to settle on something, but as the pages increased, my coughing worsened and before long undermined my resolve.

It was difficult to sleep for the coughing. I'd wake with spasms, every few hours, bathed in sweat. There was an array of prepared cough medicines I tried, which did nothing. Yorkshire Ann promised a cure with vinegar, garlic, cayenne pepper, lemon juice, and honey, which she prepared on the stove in the stillroom, but it just made me throw up. Fits of coughing were making it almost impossible for me to scale even the most benign stairs, let alone a ladder. It got to a point where even the slightest physical exertion would result in a breathless seizure, and I'd expectorate blobs of blood-tinged bile. Hotel guests covered their mouths with handkerchiefs as I passed, and finally the hotel's owner had a conference with Mrs. Newell.

"I'm afraid that coughing of yours has to stop!" Mrs. Newell said to me. Smoke from her Woodbine poured through her nostrils, filling the stillroom air above us where the laundry lines ran.

I tried to stop the coughing. I tried to will the cough away. But my efforts just seemed to exacerbate it. My face reddened, my eyes grew hot, my vision blurred.

"Perhaps you need to pack in the weed," Mrs. Newell offered, crossing her thin legs contemplatively. She hadn't noticed that I wasn't smoking; that I hadn't been able to take a drag for weeks. "I pretty well have," I exhaled in chokes.

"I see," Mrs. Newell said gravely, knowing that she and I shared a love of the weed, that I had once been almost as obsessive a chain-smoker as she. "Well, my girl, I'm afraid you'll have to see a doctor!"

I didn't have a doctor of my own in Ilfracombe. Until this cough, there'd been no reason to see one. Mrs. Newell had a word with another maid, Mrs. Wells. Wellsy, as I called her, a forty-something woman, round as she was tall, was a virtual inmate at the North Devon health clinic due to her kidney stones and chronic gallbladder problems.

"Ask to see Dr. Witmot," she advised. "He's handsome and smells nice and has very warm hands." She said this as I was trying to stop coughing long enough to strip a bed. "Warm hands on a doctor are essential," she added. But I didn't get Dr. Witmot.

A receptionist called me into an examination room. The room looked directly out onto the high street. There were no curtains at the window. People passing peered in. Between chokes and gulps, I peered back. A doctor who resembled a pig entered the room waving a file folder; presumably it contained the information I'd filled in at the reception desk. He snorted, then he told me to take off my shirt.

I choked and sputtered, pointed at the window and the people walking past.

"Come now," the doctor said, "you can't be that modest!" He set the folder down and moved toward me, as if he were going to help me overcome my modesty. I crossed my arms over my chest.

"Come now," he repeated, with impatience. "Take your shirt off! I don't have all day."

The stethoscope swung from his throat like a wrecking ball. His pink face was infusing red. He lifted the folder again and shook it.

"No." I choked, defiantly. "Forget it! I'm going."

The battle was making me cough and retch and choke all the more, and as I stood to leave, I felt the floor slip from under me. There was a skirmish of movement, the doctor trotting away; I couldn't breathe. For a moment, everything went dark. Tears poured down my cheeks; I spat up something that looked like a brown heart. The coughing stopped. I breathed. I breathed again. I breathed again.

"Tuberculosis," the doctor said triumphantly. He had gone and collected a nurse, and now stood over me with his pronouncement witnessed, and my folder tap, tap, tapping on his metal desk.

"What?" I felt another coughing fit begin to rumble.

"Tuberculosis," he repeated, as if speaking to someone who was brain-dead. "You're in the right occupation for it, a cleaner, aren't you?" He shook the folder at me.

I broke down sobbing. I couldn't stop myself from sobbing. Sobbing and hacking. Tuberculosis. That was serious and I was only seventeen.

"You're pregnant, aren't you?" the doctor fired.

"Pregnant?" I could barely say it for sobbing and coughing.

"If you're not pregnant, then why are you crying?" he asked.

"Tuberculosis," I huffed.

"Oh that," the doctor said. "Well, you're in the right occupation for it."

I didn't know then, and it would be years before I'd learn, of all the famous writers who'd succumbed to tuberculosis. Writers such as Anton Chekhov, Anne and Emily Brontë, Elizabeth Barrett Browning, Franz Kafka, John Keats, George Orwell, and Robert Louis Stevenson. Writers I had not yet read and knew nothing of, who'd sat day after day, toiling in the filth and dust of humanity. Such knowledge would have mitigated my misery, but instead, my solace came from quite another source.

I was sent to the hospital in Bideford for x-rays. On my way to the bus stop, I met Yorkshire Ann. Her face was wet with tears also, and I noticed she had a very black and swollen eye.

"It's George," she said, as though something terrible had happened to him. "He got angry with me and broke the window in our flat. If I don't get it fixed, we'll be turfed out. Can you loan us twenty quid?" She covered her eye with her hand to stop my staring.

I actually had twenty quid on me. It was tip money I'd been hoarding—money I'd intended to deposit in my building society account, money that would get me to a writers' workshop in the summer. I was going to make the deposit after I saw the doctor, but then I realized I'd need some of the money to get to Bideford, and now I saw that I really needed the money to give to Ann.

"Here you go," I said, choking, and handed her a small brown paper packet.

"You're a love," she said, counting each note, folding it, and shoving it down her blouse and into her bra.

"Don't mention it," I said.

"By the way," Ann asked, "what did the doctor say? Are you going to live?" She had that pixie grin on her face. A pixie with a black eye, I thought. A pixie who'd toppled off her mushroom.

"Who knows," I responded.

"Oh, you'll survive, I imagine. You've got lots of life ahead of you. A whole wonderful life. Wait a bit...you'll see."

ABOUT THE AUTHOR

Madeline Sonik is a teacher, writer, and editor. Her work has been published extensively in journals, magazines, and anthologies. Her latest books include *Stone Sightings* (poetry), *Arms* (a novel), *Drying the Bones* (stories), and *Belinda and the Dustbunnys* (children's novel). She has an MFA in Creative Writing and a PhD in Education, both from UBC. She has also been the recipient of numerous awards, prizes, and fellowships for her writing. She currently teaches at the University of Victoria.